ETHICS AND LEADERSHIP

Putting Theory Into Practice

Importance of Values • Conflict in Values • The Good Life •
Ethical Systems • Leadership Styles • What Should Be Done

William D. Hitt

 **BATTELLE PRESS**

Columbus • Richland

Library of Congress Cataloging-in-Publication Data

Hitt, William D.
  Ethics and leadership: putting theory into
practice / William D. Hitt.

        p.   cm.
  Includes bibliographical references.
  ISBN 0-935470-52-2 : $24.95
  1. Business ethics.   2. Management — Moral and
ethical aspects.   3. Industry — Social aspects.
4. Leadership.   I. Title
HF5387.H58   1990   89-37967
                                             CIP

Printed in the United States of America.

Battelle Press
505 King Avenue
Columbus, Ohio 43201-2693
614-424-6393
1-800-451-3543

For Diane

Acknowledgments

I have many people to thank for helping to make this book a reality. It is not possible to acknowledge all of them, but I would like to name a special few.

I am indebted to the great thinkers whose ideas have helped form the theoretical base of the text. Included are these philosophers: Karl Jaspers, John Stuart Mill, Immanuel Kant, Jean Jacques Rousseau, and Martin Buber. Also included are these contributors to the field of leadership: Machiavelli, Max Weber, Peter Drucker, James Mac-Gregor Burns, and Warren Bennis.

Without naming them individually, I would like to acknowledge the managers who have participated in my Ethics and Leadership seminar. When the manuscript was in the form of a seminar syllabus, it was these persons who sharpened my efforts in translating theory into practice.

A number of colleagues took the time to review the manuscript and offered me many valuable suggestions for making it better. I am greatly indebted to these persons: Pat Bettin, Cameron Fincher, Paul Minus, John Neale, Gerry Robinson, and Dave Snediker. This acknowledgment is not intended to imply that these reviewers endorse everything included in the book. Nor is it intended to imply that they should be held accountable for the book's shortcomings.

There are two other very special contributors to the total effort. I want to thank my secretary, Gwen Burton, for typing the manuscript. And I thank Yvonne Burry for the superb editing of the manuscript.

To each and to all of the above persons, I am grateful.

Contents

Preface

It is most important that leader-managers be aware of their considerable influence on the ethical conduct of their people. To this end, the threefold purpose of *Ethics and Leadership* is to help managers and future managers (1) understand ethics, (2) make ethical decisions, and (3) promote ethical conduct on the part of their people.

This book is addressed to anyone who is interested in the subject of ethics and leadership. Included in the intended audience are practicing managers, teachers of management, and students of management. The book may be used in at least three different ways: as a reading for self-development, as a text for an ethics seminar for practicing managers, or as a text for a business ethics course at the college level.

The book is designed to bring about *a genuine learning experience* on the part of the reader. For this reason, it cannot be merely skimmed; it must be studied.

After you have finished reading each chapter, I hope that you will take the time to complete the appropriate exercise in the Appendix. You may be certain that this active involvement will enhance the learning process.

Please appreciate that what is presented in *Ethics and Leadership* does not claim to be *the* truth; rather, it is *a* truth. It is intended to serve as a framework that will assist you in developing your own views — your own truth — about ethics and leadership. If this intention can be realized, then the endeavor will be considered successful.

ETHICS AND LEADERSHIP

Putting Theory Into Practice

Introduction

> The leader is responsible for the set of ethics or norms that govern the behavior of people in the organization. Leaders set the moral tone.
>
> Warren Bennis and Burt Nanus
Leaders[13, p.186]

Ethics and leadership go hand-in-hand. An ethical environment is conducive to effective leadership, and effective leadership is conducive to ethics. Effective leadership is a consequence of ethical conduct, and ethical conduct is a consequence of effective leadership. Ethics and leadership function as both cause and effect.

The important relation between leadership and ethics is illustrated in Figure 1, which highlights a significant cause-and-effect chain.

Beginning the chain of causal relations is the role of the leader, because leaders are the persons who influence others. Leaders do this in a number of ways: through their ability to acquire power and use

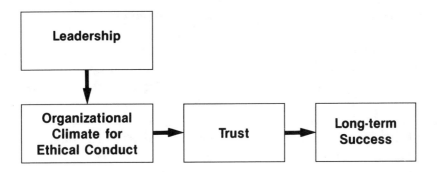

Figure 1.   A framework for leadership and ethics.

the power to achieve worthwhile ends; through their vision and their ability to transform vision into action; and through their enthusiasm and their ability to empower others. Indeed, leaders have influence. In the words of one writer, rather than say that an effective leader is one who casts a *shadow* on the organization, it is more meaningful to say that an effective leader is one who casts a *light* on the organization.

This light helps establish the organizational climate for ethical conduct. The organizational climate refers to "how we do things around here"— the ground rules that determine proper and improper conduct on the part of the organization's members. These ground rules may or may not exist in written form; nevertheless, they do exist and are communicated through words, actions, and impression. The leaders of an organization are the principal agents in establishing an organizational climate and determining whether it promotes or inhibits ethical conduct on the part of the organization's members.

Assuming that leadership is conducive to an organizational climate promoting ethical conduct, then the direct effect is the building of *trust*. Thus, we agree with those astute observers of organizational behavior who view trust as the "miracle ingredient"— the bond that holds the organization together. Without this bond, the organization becomes an assemblage of diverse individuals going their separate ways and promoting their own interests. But *with* the bond, great things can happen in the form of small miracles. And here we can agree with the Gestalt theorists when they stress that the organizational whole is greater than the sum of its membership.

This leads to the final link in the chain: long-term success as an outgrowth of trust. An organization's long-term success can be defined in terms of its productivity, financial performance, the satisfaction of stakeholders, or simply the achievement of its stated mission. Whatever the case, this long-term success is influenced greatly by trust among the organization's members and between the organization's members and all other stakeholders (i.e., those parties having an interest in the success of the organization).

Trust alone will not guarantee long-term success, and an unknown fraction of organizations may achieve long-term success without generating trust. What we are dealing with here are probabilities: we can state with considerable confidence that, everything else equal, those organizations that generate trust are much more likely to achieve long-term success than those organizations that fail to generate trust.

To repeat: leaders are persons who are able to influence others; this influence helps to establish the organizational climate for ethical conduct; the ethical conduct generates trust; and trust contributes substantially to the long-term success of the organization. While this argument may appear obvious to many, it nevertheless is a beneficial point of departure for the larger argument that follows.

The importance of leadership on the ethical conduct of followers can be appreciated if we consider the considerable elasticity of ethical conduct. Rather than view ethical conduct in terms of a dichotomy — ethical or unethical — it is much more realistic to view it in terms of a continuum. And in many situations it is helpful to think of ethical conduct on a 1-to-10 scale. In the everyday world, we find that individuals vary among themselves in their ethical conduct all the way from "1" to "10." But even more important to the subject at hand, we find that even the same individual, under different circumstances, may vary considerably in his or her ethical conduct.

The basic question, then, is what are the circumstances that will cause a particular individual to fluctuate on the ethics scale? It seems clear that an individual's nodal point on the scale is determined greatly by background — family, church, friends. But the day-to-day variation from the nodal point is influenced by current causal factors. What are these factors?

The results of research studies demonstrate that the ethical conduct of individuals in organizations is influenced greatly by their leaders. For some persons, the influence of the leader may be minimal while, for others, the influence may be substantial.

This claim is not exaggerated; it is well supported by research. The findings of Stanley Milgram's research on obedience, for example, make it clear that large numbers of people will act unethically when encouraged by others.*

In his paper, "A Psychology of Evil," David Myers provides us with a capsule summary of Milgram's findings:

> The clearest example (that large numbers of people will commit evil with remarkable ease under obedience) is Stanley Milgram's obedience experiments. Faced with an imposing, close-at-hand commander, sixty-five percent of

---

*See Stanley Milgram's *Obedience to Authority*. New York: Harper and Row, 1974.

> his adult subjects fully obeyed instructions. On command,
> they would deliver what appeared to be traumatizing elec-
> tric shocks to a screaming innocent victim in an adjacent
> room. These were regular people—a mix of blue-collar,
> white-collar and professional men. They despised their task.
> Yet obedience took precedence over their own moral sense.[92]

Considering the undue stress placed on the naive subjects who served as "teachers," one may question Milgram's ethics. But consider-ing the fact that the research design was replicated by experimenters in different parts of the world—all yielding essentially the same results—we cannot deny the findings. Other research substantiates our point: *leaders have considerable influence on the ethical con-duct of followers.*

Thus, it is most important that leader-managers be aware of their considerable influence on the ethical conduct of their people—and act accordingly. To this end, the leader-manager needs to do three things: (1) achieve an understanding of ethics; (2) serve as a role model in making ethical decisions; and (3) develop and implement a plan of action for promoting ethical conduct on the part of his or her staff.

To help meet these needs, a comprehensive and practical approach to ethics is proposed. We will call this comprehensive approach an "Encompassing theory of ethics." And we will outline an approach for translating the theory into action. Our theme throughout will be "putting theory into practice."

I

Importance of Values

Our values are so much an intrinsic part of our lives and behavior that we are often unaware of them — or, at least, we are unable to think about them clearly and articulately. Yet our values, along with other factors, clearly determine our choices, as can be proved by presenting individuals with equally "reasonable" alternative possibilities and comparing the choices they make. Some will choose one course, others another, and each will feel that his or her election is the rational one

William Guth and Renato Tagiuri
"Personal Values and Corporate Strategy"[48]

The Nature of Values • Importance of Values to End Results • Importance of Values to the Organization • Importance of Values to Society • Importance of Values to the Individual • Summing Up

---

THE NATURE OF VALUES

Ethics and values are closely connected. We begin our exploration of ethics and leadership by considering the nature of values.

Values enter into practically every decision a manager makes. Consider the following examples:

James decides to purchase the more expensive of the two computers. I ask him, "Why?" He replies, "I decided on the more expensive of the two because that company will give me better service. I *value* service."

Florence decides to extend a job offer to Sarah rather than Paul,

5

even though Paul has three years more experience than Sarah. I ask her, "Why?" She replies, "I believe Sarah is the more honest of the two. I *value* honesty."

William decides to delay submitting the final report to the client, even though he may be criticized for tardiness. I ask him, "Why?" He replies, "The report in its present form is not up to my standards of quality. I would rather take the heat on a late report than on poor quality. I *value* quality."

Martha decides to change the organizational structure of her department from a functional structure to a matrix structure, even though the change will lead to greater complexity and more confusion. I ask her, "Why?" She replies, "I realize that I will be creating some problems, but I am convinced that we will be able to achieve better teamwork. I *value* teamwork."

And so it goes. *Values enter into practically every decision a manager makes.*

Even with the omnipresence of values in our everyday lives, we still find it difficult to "get a handle" on them. Values are real yet fluffy. Idealists might say that values are the "most real" thing in the world: they lie within us; they help define who we are; they provide guidance for decision making. Nevertheless, values are difficult to comprehend. What are they? How do they come into being? Are they fixed or modifiable? How do they *actually* affect decision making? These are basic questions that must be addressed.

It is much easier to "get a handle" on facts than on values. It is a fact that one computer will cost thousands more than the other. It is a fact that Paul has three years more experience than Sarah. It is a fact that the report was submitted two weeks late. And it is a fact that a matrix structure is more complex than a functional structure. These are facts we can deal with. But how do we deal with values such as service, honesty, quality, and teamwork?

Even though the nature of values and the role of values in our everyday lives are difficult to comprehend, we can agree that they are the bedrock of ethics. According to *Webster's Dictionary*, ethics is defined as "a set of moral principles or values." A set of values is what guides a person's life, and any description of a person's ethics would have to revolve around his or her values. Ethics and values go hand-in-hand.

What, then, is a value? In *The Nature of Human Values*, Milton Rokeach defines a *value* as "an enduring belief that a specific mode of conduct or end-state of existence is personally or socially preferable to an opposite or converse mode of conduct or end-state of existence." He defines a *value system* as "an enduring organization of beliefs concerning preferable modes of conduct or end-states of existence along a continuum of relative importance."[104, p.5]

There are several key points in these two definitions. First, values are beliefs; they are not facts. Second, values are enduring; they are not transient. (But this does not mean that they are "fixed.") Third, values provide guidance with respect to two aspects of our lives: our mode of conduct (or personal behavior) and our desired end-state of existence (or personal goals). Other definitions of values are presented in the literature, but most are consistent with that proposed by Rokeach.

Rokeach also presents some clear examples of both terminal values (end-state values) and instrumental values (modes of conduct). These are shown in Figure 2 and Figure 3. Terminal values such as a sense of accomplishment, a world at peace, and social recognition may be viewed as *ends* toward which one is striving. Instrumental values such as ambition, broadmindedness, and competence may be viewed as *means* that one will employ to achieve the ends. A unified value system would be one in which the ends and the means are consistent and mutually reinforcing. For example, most would agree that a set of values that included the terminal values of "true friendship" and "mature love" and the instrumental values of "loving" and "forgiving" would be considered all of a piece.

To help clarify your own values, you may find it useful to reflect on these two sets of values in terms of *their relative importance to you*. First, study carefully the list of values presented in Figure 2. Select the five terminal values that are most important to you and the five that are least important. Then proceed to do the same with the 18 instrumental values in Figure 3.

Now for the analysis. Write down the most important values that you have selected from each set. Then answer these questions: Do the two sets of preferred values form homogeneous clusters? Do the instrumental values support the terminal values? What kind of person is described in terms of these 10 values? No small exercise — but a useful one.

Effective leader-managers will have a good understanding of their system of values. This understanding will include knowing the nature of the values, their degree of resilience, and what role they play in

1	A COMFORTABLE LIFE	A prosperous life
2	AN EXCITING LIFE	A stimulating, active life
3	A SENSE OF ACCOMPLISHMENT	Lasting contribution
4	A WORLD AT PEACE	Free of war and conflict
5	A WORLD OF BEAUTY	Beauty of nature and the arts
6	EQUALITY	Brotherhood, equal opportunity for all
7	FAMILY SECURITY	Taking care of loved ones
8	FREEDOM	Independence, free choice
9	HAPPINESS	Contentedness
10	INNER HARMONY	Freedom from inner conflict
11	MATURE LOVE	Sexual and spiritual intimacy
12	NATIONAL SECURITY	Protection from attack
13	PLEASURE	An enjoyable, leisurely life
14	SALVATION	Saved, eternal life
15	SELF-RESPECT	Self-esteem
16	SOCIAL RECOGNITION	Respect, admiration
17	TRUE FRIENDSHIP	Close companionship
18	WISDOM	A mature understanding of life

Rokeach: *The Nature of Human Values,* p. 359
Reprinted with permission (104)

Figure 2.   Terminal values.

guiding day-to-day decisions. In essence, this is what is meant by "values clarification."

In addition to achieving clarification of his or her own system of values, the leader-manager needs to understand values in much broader contexts. This includes knowing how values influence the choice of end results, what role they play in the organization, what role they play in the larger society, and what role they play in the

1	AMBITIOUS	Hard-working, aspiring
2	BROADMINDED	Open-minded
3	CAPABLE	Competent, effective
4	CHEERFUL	Lighthearted, joyful
5	CLEAN	Neat, tidy
6	COURAGEOUS	Standing up for your beliefs
7	FORGIVING	Willing to pardon others
8	HELPFUL	Working for the welfare of others
9	HONEST	Sincere, truthful
10	IMAGINATIVE	Daring, creative
11	INDEPENDENT	Self-reliant, self-sufficient
12	INTELLECTUAL	Intelligent, reflective
13	LOGICAL	Consistent, rational
14	LOVING	Affectionate, tender
15	OBEDIENT	Dutiful, respectful
16	POLITE	Courteous, well-mannered
17	RESPONSIBLE	Dependable, reliable
18	SELF-CONTROLLED	Restrained, self-disciplined

Rokeach: *The Nature of Human Values*, p. 361
Reprinted with permission (104).

Figure 3. Instrumental values.

life of an individual. This is a large order, and at least a cursory review of the role of values in these four areas is needed.

IMPORTANCE OF VALUES TO END RESULTS

Most managers understand and appreciate the importance of performance, which often is the hallmark of their success. And many would agree with Drucker's relevant dictum:

> The focus of the organization must be on *performance.* The
> first requirement of the spirit of organization is high per-
> formance standards, for the group as well as for each in-
> dividual. The organization must inculcate in itself the habit
> of achievement. But performance does not mean "success
> every time." Performance is rather a "batting average." It
> will, indeed it must, have room for mistakes and even for
> failures. What performance has no room for is complacency
> and low standards.[32, p.456]

Without a proper focus on performance, managers are caught
in the Activity Trap. They gear their efforts to work rather than
results. George Odiorne, the well known expert on management by
objectives, pinpoints the pitfalls associated with the Activity Trap:

1. "People get so enmeshed in activity that they lose sight of the
   purpose of their work.
2. People caught in the Activity Trap diminish in capability rather
   than grow.
3. The Activity Trap originates at the top of organizations and
   extends to the lowest levels.
4. Organizations that have become Activity Traps kill motivation of people working in them.
5. Most problems don't get solved in activity-centered organizations, and some problems get worse.
6. Activity-centered managers avoid reality by converting it into
   something else."[94, p.301]

I recall listening to a manager complaining about a two-hour
meeting that he attended every Monday. These meetings generally
were not well conducted and apparently had no direct relevance to
his job. He felt that the meetings were a complete waste of time. When
I asked him *why* he attended the meetings, he replied, "Well, I've
always attended the meetings." And so it goes. Many managers do
indeed get caught up in the Activity Trap and lose sight of what their
jobs are all about — namely, to focus on performance.

A powerful tool for coping with the Activity Trap is "managing
for results." This notion was introduced to the management world
by Peter Drucker back in the mid-1950s and has had a profound impact on management thought and practice from that time up to the
present.

To appreciate the full import of managing for results (or "management by objectives" as it is typically known), one must appreciate

the nature of American management thought and practice prior to the mid-1950s. During those years managers tended to focus only on inputs and activity. Inputs included capital, labor, and materials. Activity included procedures, efforts, means. (Where are outputs?) But management by objectives enlarged the equation to include outputs — objectives, results, ends. With this addition, the new management thinking encompassed input, activity, and outputs as an integrated system.

The traditional management by objectives process is fairly well agreed upon by the experts on the subject. Typically, this is a top-down approach that begins with upper management formulating annual objectives for the organization as a whole. This is then followed by subordinate departments, sections, and groups formulating their objectives in the light of the organizational objectives. Next, each manager meets with each of his or her people on a one-to-one basis to mutually agree on each staff member's annual performance objectives. Progress toward the objectives is reviewed informally throughout the year and then formally at the end of the year. Some version of this strategy has been implemented in large numbers of organizations.

For many managers, such a way of managing has become a way of life. Some will even ask, "What other way of managing is there?"

Without getting carried away with the elegance and power of management by objectives, we can affirm that it has both strengths and weaknesses. As a concept, it is difficult to criticize, because it is simply a rational approach to management. But as a practice, it is found wanting: it has sometimes led to a mechanization of the management function and a rigidity that has stifled creativity and innovation. Nevertheless, there are true believers who would avow that management by objectives is the most significant innovation in management since the publication in 1911 of Frederick Taylor's classic book, *Principles and Methods of Scientific Management* (New York: Harper & Brothers).

Management by objectives as a systematic process of management is granted its strengths *and* its limitations. Even the critics who charge that the process is too mechanistic find it hard to question the utility of having clearly defined objectives and directing one's activities toward these objectives.

The point to be emphasized is: *managers need a set of values to guide them in the selection of objectives.* The world is so open: we are faced with innumerable possibilities in the selection of objectives toward which to direct our efforts. How do we choose? Consider the following examples of basic decisions facing managers.

Should we focus on efficiency or effectiveness? In the words of Drucker, "Efficiency is concerned with doing things right and effectiveness is doing the right things."[32, p.45] Building on this idea, Bennis and Nanus make this distinction between managers and leaders: "Managers are people who do things right and leaders are people who do the right thing."[13, p.21] As conscientious *leader-managers*, don't we want to do both? But in terms of priorities, suppose we are forced to choose. Which way should we go? We need direction.

Should we focus on short-term results or long-term results? If we are concerned only with this coming year's bottom line, our objectives and strategy will be different from those that we would pursue for long-term results. Investment in staff development and facilities, for example, would be of considerable importance to long-term objectives but would be of relatively little importance to short-term objectives. We need guidance.

Should we focus on immediate profit or market share? If the emphasis is on maximizing profits for this coming fiscal year, then we probably will direct our attention to our existing customers, and announce a modest increase in prices. But if the emphasis is on achieving greater market share, we probably will invest heavily in marketing to new customers and may even lower our prices. We need to know which way to go.

Should we focus on productivity or innovation? If we are to be evaluated only on the number of units manufactured, then we will concentrate on producing our existing products in large number. But if we are to be evaluated on the number of new products developed, then we will give more attention to innovation. Which should we choose?

Should we focus on facilities development or people development? Our facilities are in desperate need of refurbishing. But many of our people are in desperate need of training. If we focus on the facilities, the improvements will be readily apparent. But if we focus on staff development, the improvements may not be so readily apparent. But, then again, maybe we are kidding ourselves. And some contend that we should do both. That is nice in theory, but we have limited resources. Which way do we turn?

With regard to managing our projects, should we focus on quality, schedule, or budget? We realize, of course, that our clients want all three. But our project leaders continue to present this claim: "On any given project we can optimize any two of the criteria, but not all three. Tell us which two and we will act accordingly." These project leaders need guidance.

And so it goes. Other examples would underscore our need for guidance in determing priorities and formulating objectives. This guidance should be in the form of clearly articulated values: guiding beliefs that communicate what we stand for and what is important to us.

Managers should make certain that the values guide the selection of objectives and not allow the objectives to dictate the selection of values. In everyday parlance, "The horse should come before the cart." A practical way to achieve this desirable state of affairs is to include a review of values as an integral part of every planning activity. And it should be a step that occurs early in the process, be it in the development of a five-year strategic plan, a one-year operational plan, or a six-month project plan.

Giving due consideration to basic values in every planning activity will provide a significant part of the guidance needed in determining priorities and formulating of objectives. And this will lead to better management.

The need for a clear set of values in selecting end results is evident. Equally evident is the need for a clear set of values to guide the organization as a whole.

IMPORTANCE OF VALUES TO THE ORGANIZATION*

The importance of corporate values is elucidated by Thomas Watson, Jr. in this IBM credo:

> I firmly believe that any organization, in order to survive and achieve success, must have a sound set of beliefs on which it premises all its policies and actions.
>
> Next, I believe that the most important factor in corporate success is faithful adherence to those beliefs.
>
> And finally, I believe that if an organization is to meet the challenge of a changing world, it must be prepared to

---

*This section is reproduced from *The Leader-Manager* by William D. Hitt. Columbus: Battelle Press, 1988.

> change everything about itself except those beliefs as it
> moves through corporate life.[97, p.184]

Watson was referring specifically to this set of beliefs:

- **Respect for the individual** — to respect the dignity and rights of each person in the organization.
- **Customer service** — to give the best customer service of any company in the world.
- **Excellence** — to hold the conviction that any organization should pursue all tasks with the objective of accomplishing them in a superior way.

Every organization is guided by certain beliefs or values. These values communicate to all members "what we stand for" and "what is important to us." Whether the values are explicit or only implicit, they constitute the essence of the organization's credo and management philosophy. Values are the soul of the organization.

One sign of a healthy organizational culture is congruence between the organization's statement of values and the daily behavior of its members. Conversely, one sign of an organizational culture in trouble is lack of congruence between the organization's statement of values and the daily behavior of its members. It is clear that every enterprise needs an explicit statement of organizational values and the witnessing of these values in the day-to-day actions of its members — that is, harmony in values.

What is meant by "harmony in values"? We mean essentially two things: first, the values of the organization are all of a piece and, second, the values of the organization and the behavior of its members are consistent.

Suppose that you are listening to an orchestra that is not in harmony. After listening to the discordance for a few moments, you become aware that something is terribly amiss. It appears that the musicians are not following the same musical score. It even appears that some members are not following any score at all. What is most disconcerting is that the leader sometimes follows the score and sometimes does not. Even the score itself seems to be incongruous — a crazy mixture of classical, jazz, and hard rock. How long would you remain at this bizarre event? Probably not very long. Only a masochist would remain.

If we equate "musical score" and "organizational values," this situation is not unlike that which is found in some organizations. Just as the score is important to the performance of the members of the orchestra, the values are important to the performance of the members of an organization.

We do not have to look far to find examples of discordance in organizational values. Readily apparent are these examples:

1. Incongruity between the statement of organizational values and the real understanding of these values on the part of the members.
2. Incongruity between the values of one unit and those of another in the same organization.
3. Incongruity between the statement of organizational values and the behavior of the organization's leaders.

The existence of any one of these incongruities would be reason for concern. An organization plagued with all three simultaneously would be considered a sick organization — or at least a sick organizational culture.

For each manager there is a clear challenge: do whatever is reasonably possible to assure a high degree of congruence between the organization's guiding beliefs and the members' daily beliefs. First, the guiding beliefs must be clearly communicated to all members of the organization. Next, these guiding beliefs must be put into practice on a daily basis.

Assuming success in this endeavor, one can expect the following desirable outcomes.

Harmony in values will provide a sense of common direction for all staff and guidelines for their daily behavior. We have suggested that organizational values are to the staff what the musical score is to the musicians. Even though the staff may be talented and versatile, they still need to know what kind of music they are expected to play — classical, jazz, or hard rock. Without a clear and consistent signal on this matter, there may be a great deal of noise but little music.

Harmony in values will provide the social energy and esprit de corps that moves the organization into action. Perhaps the organization will be able to move from state A to state B merely by means of physical energy. But certainly it will move more rapidly and more successfully if the physical energy is supplemented by social energy. Social energy is generated whenever people are working together as *a community of persons with a common center.* This common center denotes the organizational values, and the radii represent the com mitment of the individual members to these organizational values. Here we find esprit de corps at its best.

Harmony in values will permit upper management to influence employee behavior without being present physically. Even if it were possible for upper management to be physically present to oversee the work of the employees, it would be undesirable from a motivational standpoint. But there is a definite way for upper management to have a profound impact on the behavior of every member of the organization at all times: by clearly communicating the values and doing everything reasonably possible to win a commitment to these values. Assuming success in this endeavor, then the organizational values will serve as the *collective conscience* for all members of the organization.

Harmony in values will provide a framework for managerial decision making. Here the organizational values serve as a *gyroscope*, an apparatus capable of maintaining the same absolute direction in space in spite of the movements of the mountings and surrounding parts. Managers make decisions day in and day out, perhaps almost every hour of each day. Effective managers make decisions in accord with a structured rationale, a rationale that is grounded in organizational values. If these managers had to create the rationale for each particular decision, they would be functioning as psychological cripples. What saves them from this malady is that their decision making is guided by organizational values.

Harmony in values will provide a sense of stability and continuity in a rapidly changing environment. Most human beings have a basic need for stability and continuity. Because large numbers of organizations are now experiencing periods of rapid change, we are even more aware of this basic human need. And it is apparent from all projections that these changes will even accelerate in the future. Many managers are sensitive to the need to help their employees maintain a reasonable level of sanity in this ever-changing world. One of the keys is to communicate the organization's values as enduring ideals. Even though the vessel is moving hither and yon across a tumultuous sea, the values will serve as a rudder.

Achieving these five desirable outcomes through harmony in values will be a major achievement. Indeed, this can spell the difference between failure and success, between despair and joy.

Thus, it is clear that an organization, to be successful, needs the guidance of a clear set of values. On a larger scale, a society — to be a society — needs the guidance of a clear set of values.

IMPORTANCE OF VALUES TO SOCIETY

What distinguishes an American from a citizen of any other country? from an Egyptian? from a Japanese? from an Australian? from a Mexican? One might respond facetiously that the American will be wearing blue jeans and a stereo headset. But more significant are the differences in basic values — the beliefs that guide one's life. This is not to imply in any way that the values of one nation are superior to those of another, but merely to highlight that there are significant differences.

In *Habits of the Heart,* Robert Bellah and his associates make special note of the role that tradition (i.e., beliefs and customs) plays in shaping our lives:

> In short, we have never been, and still are not, a collection of private individuals who, except for a conscious contract to create a minimal government, have nothing in common. Our lives make sense in a thousand ways, most of which we are unaware of, because of traditions that are centuries, if not millennia, old. It is these traditions that help us to know that it does make a difference who we are and how we treat one another.[9, p.283]

American values make us who we are. They contribute to our basic beliefs about the nature of the good life, provide us with direction, and give meaning to our lives. In essence, they help us form an identity. Collectively, the values shape what is called a "national character."

In addition to shaping the national character, the values serve as the watershed for the establishment of particular civil laws. Where did our laws come from? On what basis were they created? To a considerable extent, the laws are rooted in traditional American values and, over time, as the values change, the laws are modified. In the words of Rousseau, "The particular laws are only the curve of the arch, while the morals and customs are the keystone."[106, p.49]

That American values are the keystone is fully understood by many candidates for political office. I recall hearing a candidate for the U.S. presidency make a commitment to "basic American values." His promise to the TV audience went something like this: "I am committed to upholding traditional American values. I firmly believe in these values and, as President, it will be my duty to protect them and promote them. It also will be my duty to secure these values for future generations."

After hearing the opposing candidate espouse essentially the same message, I took it upon myself to make a search for a listing of American values. My search covered some very rich resource documents: the Declaration of Independence, the U. S. Constitution, works by Thomas Paine, several American history books, and speeches and papers by past presidents. Nowhere did I find a listing of what might be called "American values." But the search was not for naught. It helped me delineate what I consider to be basic American values. These ten basic American values are listed in Figure 4, with supporting quotations from intellectual and political leaders presented in the ten pages that follow.

Read this material on American values carefully. Mull it over and reflect on its significance. Then decide for yourself: Is this an adequate representation of American values? If not, what changes would

---

1.   DEMOCRACY

2.   JUSTICE

3.   HUMAN RIGHTS

4.   EQUALITY

5.   FREEDOM

6.   RESPONSIBILITY

7.   REASON

8.   DIVERSITY OF OPINION

9.   QUALITY OF LIFE

10.   WORLD PEACE

Figure 4. American values.

you propose? I believe that you will find this to be a stimulating and fruitful exercise. Throughout the exercise, you should consider the role that these values — either my list or your own — has played in shaping your life. To what extent have the values determined what you are and who you are? And also important for your consideration: How does this set of values differ from what might be found in another society? In which societies might they be very similar? And in which societies might they be quite different?

1. Democracy

I believe in the United States of America as a government of the people, by the people, for the people; whose just powers are derived from the consent of the governed; a democracy in a republic; a sovereign nation of many sovereign states; a perfect Union, one and inseparable; established upon the principles of freedom, equality, justice, and humanity for which American patriots sacrificed their lives and fortunes.
— *William Tyler Page*

The democratic theory is that the majority will have a vision of the common good and act in the best interest of the particular community. The aims and objectives, as well as the procedures for attaining them, will change from time to time as new needs arise and as the wisdom of the people grows. Certainly the wisdom of the people is likely to be a better guide over the years than the vision of a ruler or family.
— *William Douglas*

2. Justice

The Declaration of Independence affirms that all human beings are equal in one fundamental respect. They are all equally human. What has this affirmation of human equality to do with justice? The answer is to be found in the complaint we have all heard uttered by even very young children: that they are being treated unjustly or unfairly when one of their siblings receives treatment of which they themselves are deprived.   *— Mortimer Adler*

Justice gives rise to a threefold division: (1) the justice to be done by the state in relation to its people or by the government in relation to the governed; (2) the justice to be done with regard to the relation of one citizen or group of citizens to another citizen or group of citizens; and (3) the justice to be done by citizens in relations to the community as a whole and in service to its common good.   *— Mortimer Adler*

3. Human Rights

Every generation is equal in rights to the generations
which preceded it, by the same rule that every individual is born equal in rights with his contemporaries.
                                                    —*Thomas Paine*

We hold these truths to be self-evident: that all men
are created equal; that they are endowed by their
Creator with certain unalienable rights; that among
these are life, liberty, and the pursuit of happiness;
that, to secure these rights, governments are instituted
among men, deriving their just powers from the consent of the governed .... —*Thomas Jefferson*

4. Equality

Fourscore and seven years ago our fathers brought forth on this continent a new nation, conceived in liberty and dedicated to the proposition that all men are created equal!   —*Abraham Lincoln*

I wish to see all unjust and unnecessary discrimination everywhere abolished, and that the time may come when all our inhabitants of every colour and discrimination shall be free and equal partakers of our political liberty.   —*John Jay*

5. Freedom

In the future days, which we seek to make secure, we look forward to a world founded upon four essential human freedoms: the first is freedom of speech and expression, everywhere in the world. The second is freedom of every person to worship God in his own way, everywhere in the world. The third is freedom from want, everywhere in the world. The fourth is freedom from fear anywhere in the world.

— Franklin Delano Roosevelt

When we let freedom ring, when we let it ring from every village and hamlet, from every state and every city, we will be able to speed up the day when all of God's children, black men and white men, Jews and Gentiles, Protestants and Catholics, will be able to join hands and sing the words of that old Negro spiritual, "Free at Last! Free at last! Thank God almighty, we are free at last!"

— Martin Luther King, Jr.

6. Responsibility

I believe it is my duty to my country to love it, to support its Constitution; to obey its laws; to respect its flag and to defend it against all enemies.

—William Tyler Page

My fellow Americans: ask not what your country can do for you; ask what you can do for your country.

—John Kennedy

7. Reason

Reason and ignorance, the opposites of each other, influence the great bulk of mankind. If either of these can be rendered sufficiently extensive in a country, the machinery of government goes easily on. Reason shows itself, and ignorance submits to whatever is dictated to it. —*Thomas Paine*

It rests now with ourselves alone to enjoy in peace and concord the blessings of self-government, so long denied to mankind: to show by example the sufficiency of human reason for the care of human affairs and that the will of the majority, the natural law of every society, is the only sure guardian of the rights of man. —*Thomas Jefferson*

8. Diversity of Opinion

It is a singular anxiety which some people have that we should all think alike. Would the world be more beautiful were all our faces alike? were our tempers, our talents, our tastes, our forms, our wishes, aversions and pursuits cast exactly in the same mould? If no varieties existed in the animal, vegetable or mineral creation, but all move exactly uniform, catholic and orthodox, what a world of physical and moral monotony it would be!   —*Thomas Jefferson*

If men are to be precluded from offering their sentiments on a matter, which may involve the most serious and alarming consequences that can invite the consideration of mankind, reason is of no use to us; the freedom of speech may be taken away, and dumb and silent may be led, like sheep to the slaughter.
                                             — *George Washington*

9. Quality of Life

If I were asked to state the great objective which Church and State are both demanding for the sake of every man and woman and child in this country, I would say that that great objective is "a more abundant life." — *Franklin Delano Roosevelt*

A strong America cannot neglect the aspirations of its citizens — the welfare of the needy, the health care of the elderly, the education of the young. For we are not developing the nation's wealth for its own sake. Wealth is the means, and the people are the end. All our material riches will avail us little if we do not use them to expand the opportunities of our people.
— *John Kennedy*

---

10. World Peace

We have learned that we cannot live alone, at peace; that our own well-being is dependent on the well-being of other nations far away. We have learned that we must live as men, and not as ostriches, nor as dogs in the manger. We have learned to be citizens of the world, members of the human community.

— Franklin Delano Roosevelt

Peace does not rest in the charters and covenants alone. It lies in the hearts and minds of all people. And . . . no act, no pact, no treaty, no organization can hope to preserve it without the support and the whole-hearted commitment of all people.

— John Kennedy

IMPORTANCE OF VALUES TO THE INDIVIDUAL

Turning next to the importance of values to the individual, we should reflect on these words by Abraham Maslow:

> The human being needs a framework of values, a philosophy of life, a religion or religion-surrogate to live by and understand by, in about the same sense that he needs sunlight, calcium, or love.[81, p.206]

Indeed, every person needs a well-thought-out philosophy of life to provide direction and give meaning to life. At the core of a philosophy of life is a set of values — a set of basic beliefs that defines what a person stands for.

To illustrate the point, we will consider the lives of two hypothetical individuals. Jeremiah, as far as can be ascertained, has no well-thought-out values to guide his life. Jessica, in sharp contrast, has a clearly defined set of values to guide her life.

Jeremiah is an unfortunate human being. A 24-year-old man, he is sometimes referred to as a "drifter." Much of what he is today — or what he is not — can be traced back to his childhood. Because his parents abandoned him when he was only three years of age, he was placed with foster parents. In a period of 15 years, he lived in three different foster homes. The six different parents with whom he lived over these formative years were a rather motley group — varying considerably in their beliefs, attitudes, personalities, and life styles. Consequently, the young Jeremiah never found an anchor that he could hold onto: he had no role model who could provide him with a set of values. Today we can see the consequence of this unfavorable upbringing.

It may be incorrect to state that Jeremiah has no values, because he does have two: seeking pleasure and avoiding pain. He enjoys pleasurable experiences (such as draft beer and video games), so he seeks out those things that will give him immediate sensory gratification. And he dislikes pain, so he carefully avoids those things that will cause distressing sensations. Other than these two rock-bottom values, we can safely say that Jeremiah has no guiding beliefs.

Jeremiah may be described as a person who lacks a clear sense of identity. There is no central core that defines a self. It would not be possible for him to say, with any conviction, "I believe." And it would not be possible for him to look in the mirror and say, with any real understanding, "I." Granted there is a minimal "I" that represents this particular physical body, but beneath the skin and bones there is a deep cavity.

Because of the lack of identity, Jeremiah is found wanting with respect to a unified personality. If his acquaintances were asked to describe him, they might readily describe his physical features and what kind of car he drove, but would be hard pressed to describe him as a person. The fact of the matter is that Jeremiah is made up of a whole bunch of scattered elements, without unity and without coherence.

With regard to ethics, Jeremiah lacks clear standards for judging right and wrong. Other than the desire to seek pleasure and avoid pain, he has no criteria for judging if one action is preferable to another. Because he wants to avoid pain, he has learned from experience that it is to his advantage to abide by the law. But beyond this minimal level he has no ethical standards.

Consequently, Jeremiah is vulnerable to the buffetings of the ex-

ternal world. Day in and day out he is faced with pressures and temptations, first from one side and then from another. Lacking a clear
set of values to serve as a moral compass, he simply bounces hither
and yon as a ping pong ball.

In looking ahead, we must agree that Jeremiah's future appears
to be rather bleak. His "unexamined life" holds little promise. Here
is a human being with a reasonably sound physical body, a modicum
of intelligence, and some basic skills — but an entity without a compass. Indeed, it would be difficult to foretell where Jeremiah is
headed, how he plans to get there, or how he will end up. There is
too much uncertainty.

Standing in sharp contrast to Jeremiah is Jessica. Here is a person who "has it all together." Other than also being 24 years of age,
she has nothing in common with Jeremiah.

Jessica was blessed with a positive and nourishing childhood. She
was a respected member of a loving family that encouraged the development of basic values and the living of these values on a daily
basis.

Jessica does indeed have a set of well-thought-out values. In terms
of Rokeach's two lists of values, her terminal values are "a world at
peace" and "a sense of accomplishment." Her instrumental values are
"courage," "helpfulness," and "love." These values are a set — they are
all of a piece. They constitute her basic beliefs and serve as the guide
for her everyday life.

In contrast to Jeremiah, Jessica has a strong sense of identity.
When she says "I believe," it is said with conviction. When she looks
in the mirror and says "I," it is said with understanding and meaning.

Jessica's friends could readily describe her personality. One could
expect to hear such descriptive statements as "She is a very caring
person." . . . "She provides a helping relationship." . . . "She is a
dedicated person." We get a clear picture.

Jessica's friends also would stress that she is a person of integrity.
She has clear standards for judging right and wrong. Not that all
issues are viewed simply as black-and-white matters, but she can
clearly discern the ethical and the unethical. She knows what is
"right"— and she has the trust and respect of all who know her.

Because of her clear sense of values, Jessica is not vulnerable to
the buffetings of the external world. She is faced with many of the
same pressures and temptations faced by Jeremiah, but it is much
easier for her to deal with them. Because of her deep understanding

of her personal values and the internalization of these values in her self-being, Jessica can make most of her decisions of an ethical nature with little or no hesitation. They simply "fall in place."

In looking ahead, it would appear that Jessica has a bright future. She knows who she is and she knows what she wants to accomplish in life. Her life is guided by an internal gyroscope that is powered by deeply held beliefs. Certainly, she will have some ups and downs in life, but she will continue to move forward. In the language of Socrates, she will "live the good life."

Thus, we see here two individuals with dramatically different approaches to life. The most fundamental difference between the two is the difference in values. Jeremiah, for all intent or purpose, has no basic values to guide his life — which will result in lack of direction, randomness of activity, and unfulfilled life. Jessica, on the other hand, has a well-thought-out set of values to guide her life — which will provide her with direction, meaning, and self-fulfillment.

Undoubtedly most thoughtful individuals would agree that Jessica's path is the one to follow. Be it in our own personal development or in the education of our young people, we should be sensitive to the importance of personal values in one's life. They are the cornerstone of self-development.

SUMMING UP

To understand ethics and what influences ethical conduct, it is essential that the leader-manager understand the nature of human values — the bedrock of ethics.

Rokeach defines a *value* as an enduring belief that a specific mode of conduct or end-state of existence is personally or socially preferable to some other mode of conduct or end-state of existence. A *value system* is an enduring organization of beliefs concerning preferable modes of conduct or end-states of existence along a continuum of relative importance.

In addition to understanding their own value systems, leader-managers need to understand values in a much broader context. This includes understanding how values influence the selection of end results, what role they play in the organization, what role they play in the larger society, and what role they play in the life of an individual.

We have presented examples of values in each of these four domains:

- **End results:** productivity, effectiveness, efficiency, return on investment.
- **Organization:** respect for the individual, excellence, customer service.
- **Nation:** democracy, justice, human rights, equality, freedom, responsibility, reason, diversity of opinion, quality of life, world peace.
- **Individual:** a world at peace, a sense of accomplishment, love, helpfulness, courage.

These values serve as the foundation of our ethics. Webster's definition of ethics is "a set of moral principles or values." It then follows that an individual's personal value system provides the foundation for his or her ethics. The personal value system is what guides a person's life, and any description of a person's ethics would have to center on his or her personal value system.

The benefits of a personal value system have been delineated by George England:[37]

1. A personal value system influences a manager's perception of situations and problems he/she faces.
2. A personal value system influences a manager's decisions and solutions to problems.
3. A personal value system influences the way in which a manager looks at other individuals and groups of individuals; thus it influences interpersonal relationships.
4. A personal value system influences the perception of individual and organizational success as well as their achievement.
5. A personal value system sets the limits for the determination of what is and what is not ethical behavior by a manager.
6. A personal value system influences the extent to which a manager will accept or will resist organizational pressures.

The basic message here is expressed beautifully by Socrates:

> Every man should expend his chief thought and attention on his first principles: Are they or are they not rightly laid down? And when he has duly sifted them, all the rest will follow.[62, p.225]

II

Conflict in Values

The manager has to live with a life in which he never really gets the luxury of choosing between right and wrong. He has to decide usually between two wrongs. In any decision he makes, he hurts somebody. And that's his career. If he's too uncomfortable with that, he ought to be in some other business. Obviously he ought to be uncomfortable with it. If he isn't uncomfortable, he's not very human.

> J. Irwin Miller[39, p.202]
> *Former Chairman*
> *Cummins Engine Company*

The Nature of Dilemmas • End-Result Dilemmas • Organizational Dilemmas • Societal Dilemmas • Personal Dilemmas • Summing Up

---

THE NATURE OF DILEMMAS

Managers must make many ethical decisions. Oftentimes such decisions do not call for simple right or wrong choices. Instead, they frequently call for a decision between two wrongs, with undesirable consequences associated with both alternatives. And there are no ready-made answers in the operations manual. Ethical choices must be made in the real world of managerial decision making.

The matter of ethical dilemmas is put in perspective by Sir Adrian Cadbury:

> The rule that it is best to tell the truth often runs up against the rule that we should not hurt people's feelings un-

necessarily. There is no simple, universal formula for solving ethical problems. We have to choose from our own codes
of conduct whichever rules are appropriate to the case in
hand; the outcome of those choices makes us who we are.[27]

A framework that will help us understand the nature of ethical
dilemmas is provided by James Rest. In his book, *Moral Development*, he lists in sequential order four requirements for ethical decision making:

1. The person must be able to make some sort of interpretation
   of the particular situation in terms of what actions are possible.
2. The person must be able to make a *judgment* about which
   course of action is ethically right.
3. The person must *give priority* to ethical values above other
   personal values such that a decision is made to intend to do
   what is ethically right.
4. The person must have sufficient perseverance, ego strength,
   and implementation skills to be able to *follow through* on
   his/her intention.[103]

This sequence of steps reveals several potential problems. For
example, a person may have been able to interpret a given situation
to realize there were alternatives available (Step 1) but did not realize
that there was an ethical dimension involved in the decision (Step
2). Or the person may have been able to make a judgment about
which course of action was ethically right (Step 2) but nevertheless
did not give priority to ethical values above other personal values
(Step 3). Or finally, the individual may indeed have given priority
to ethical values above other personal values (Step 3) but did not
follow through on his or her intention (Step 4).

In addition to the ethical dilemmas encountered between any two
adjacent steps, there are potential dilemmas within a particular step.
In Step 2, for example, managers might be able *to make a judgment*
about which course of action is ethically right, but realize that this
is not the practical thing to do. Or in Step 3, they may intend to *give
priority* to ethical values over other personal values, but find themselves forced to choose between two equally attractive or equally unat-
tractive alternatives. Or in Step 4, they sincerely plan to follow
through on good intentions, but run into constraints beyond their
control.

This four-step process highlights the salient features of ethical conduct. An understanding of this process will clarify the nature of ethical dilemmas faced by managers.

Perhaps the most common dilemmas facing managers involve decisions with both an economic dimension and an ethical dimension. The economic dimension points the manager toward the bottom line of financial performance. The ethical dimension points the manager toward doing the right thing for people.

To appreciate the significance of the economic-ethical dilemma, consider the following case. You are the manager of a 12-person group. One of your best employees, who was in a serious accident, has now returned to work. Because of the nature of the injury, the employee is not very productive and is unlikely to be productive over the next 12 months. This is a single parent who is responsible for the care and feeding of two teenage daughters. The problem: you are getting increased pressure from above to improve your group's productivity. What would be your plan of action?

In considering a case such as this, it becomes apparent that a manager needs a framework for decision making that incorporates both the economic dimension and the ethical dimension. To this end, it is useful to view the economic dimension in terms of good and bad decisions, and the ethical dimension in terms of right and wrong decisions. The manager's goal, then, would be to make decisions that are both right and good.

This double distinction reminds me of the everyday language used by a farmer for whom I worked in my high school days. Old Jake would use adjectives that I thought were redundant. These were typical statements: "That was a right-good idea." ... "You did a right-good job." ... "He's a right-good worker." (He meant, of course, a "very" good idea, a "very" good job, a "very" good worker.) Indeed, it now seems that Jake had the correct approach. What we need on the part of managers are right-good decisions. Such decisions are good from an economic standpoint and right from an ethical standpoint. Thus, it should not be right *versus* good, but rather, right *and* good. This is what it is all about. Perhaps Old Jake had more wisdom than I realized at the time.

Now we can develop a framework for considering these two dimensions of decision making. In Figure 5, the horizontal axis represents the economic dimension of decision making (i.e., the goodness of decisions), and the vertical axis represents the ethical dimension (i.e., the rightness of decisions).

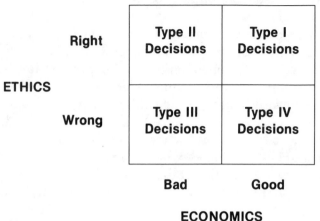

Figure 5.   Two dimensions of decision making.

It is important to appreciate that the two dimensions are defined in terms of two different sets of criteria. The economic dimension is defined in terms of criteria such as revenue, profit, return on investment, and cash flow. The ethical dimension is defined in terms of criteria such as compassion, fairness, honesty, and responsibility. The two sets represent radically different criteria. Will it be possible to achieve a rapprochement between the two? Our thesis here is that the answer is "yes."

Consider for a moment the four types of decisions revealed in the diagram. Type I decisions are high on economics, high on ethics. Type II decisions are high on ethics, low on economics. Type III decisions are low on economics, low on ethics. And Type IV decisions are high on economics, low on ethics.

We can envision four different managers who would characterize the four quadrants. Starting in the lower-left quadrant (the Type III decision maker — low on economics, low on ethics), we find an individual who should not have been placed in a management position. This was a mistake of the highest order. Then moving to the upper-left quadrant (the Type II decision maker — high on ethics, low on economics), we find a manager who may be loved as a person, as a decent human being, but not respected as a results-oriented manager. Perhaps this person could be moved out of management into some other position. Looking next at the lower-right quadrant (the Type IV decision maker — high on economics, low on ethics), we find a manager who may be successful in the short run. But because of failure to generate trust, this manager will ultimately fail. Finally, we consider the upper-right quadrant (the Type I decision maker — high on economics, high on ethics). Here we have the true leader-manager. If we were betting on which of the four managers is most likely to achieve long-term success, this is the manager on whom I would place my bet.

Building on these concepts, we will now examine conflict in values in the four spheres discussed in Chapter I. Included here are examples of end-result dilemmas, organizational dilemmas, societal dilemmas, and personal dilemmas.

In examining the 24 brief cases, the decision making framework provided by James Rest[103] should prove helpful. Focus on these questions:

1. What are the options?
2. What, if any, is the ethical dimension associated with the case?
3. Which option would you choose?
4. In implementing your option, what obstacles would you expect to encounter?

END-RESULT DILEMMAS

There is no question today that large numbers of managers throughout the U.S. and abroad are results-oriented. Such managers plan their year in terms of expected results and then gear their activities to the achievement of these results.

With regard to products and services, results-oriented managers typically focus on four distinct criteria: quality, schedule, budget, and health and safety. In reference to a particular product or service, quality may be defined as "satisfying valid requirements." Schedule refers to the timetable that is to be met. Budget refers to the amount of money that is available. And concerns about health and safety apply to the producers or providers of the product or service as well as to the recipients.

As portrayed in Figure 6, there are six potential inter-criteria conflicts: quality vs. schedule, quality vs. budget, quality vs. health and safety, schedule vs. budget, schedule vs. health and safety, and budget vs. health and safety. On the following pages, we will consider examples of each type of conflict.

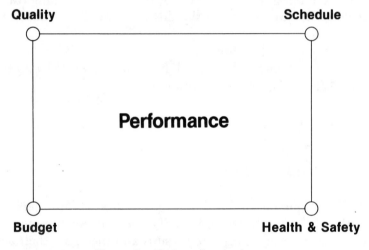

Figure 6.   End-result criteria.

1. Quality vs. Schedule

As director of marketing in a telecommunication company, you have promised a number of customers the delivery of a new telephone switching system by a certain date. The problem is that the switching system will not be at the desired level of quality by that date—but you think it can be "fixed" after it is installed. Your competition is closing in.

* * * *

This is not an unusual situation. There is always a degree of optimism when making the initial promise to the client and, in turn, establishing a formal contract. But, invariably, some unexpected "bugs" in the system cause delays.

So now you are faced with a serious dilemma. You can push ahead and install the system, which will meet the customer's schedule requirements and may keep the competition away temporarily. (But you know full well that all of the necessary debugging activities that will be required after installing the system are certain to raise the ire of your customer.) Or you can hold back on the shipment until you have the system completely debugged. (But tomorrow your chief competitor may be knocking at your customer's door, prepared to install a "fully tested" system.)

A key consideration in this case is building and maintaining trust with your client. This requires honest and open communication—and no surprises.

What would be your course of action?

2. Quality vs. Budget

You are the manager of a project that can achieve the level of quality specified in the written contract and stay within the budget. The problem is that you made an oral agreement with the client to achieve a higher level of quality. Because of some unexpected costs that have been incurred during the past three months, you now realize that achieving this higher level of quality will cause a project overrun and absorb the entire fee (profit).

* * * *

You are in a difficult situation. Some would say that you should not have made the oral agreement to achieve a higher level of quality. And they are right. But that is hindsight.

Your present predicament is to resolve the dilemma. If you focus only on satisfying your client by keeping your promise, you may have a satisfied client, but you surely will have an unhappy manager above you — the one who is concerned about cost overruns. On the other hand, if you renege on your promise in order to stay within the project budget, you are sure to have an unhappy client.

A key consideration here is the action that is required to maintain a good long-term relationship with the client.

What would be your course of action?

3. Quality vs. Health & Safety

As director of safety in an automobile manufacturing company, you are eager to begin installing air safety bags in all new cars. But you are faced with a dilemma: you are convinced that these air bags will save scores of lives in the long run, but during the early stages of development, some of the bags may inflate unexpectedly and cause accidents. These accidents could lead to subsequent lawsuits against your company.

* * * *

You are in a highly responsible position, and your decision (or recommendation) on this matter could have a profound impact on the company.

Assume that you have been involved in the development of the air safety bags from the very beginning. As a consequence, you have both a personal and a professional commitment to see these safety devices installed in every car that your company manufactures.

Here we are dealing with statistics and probabilities. If you push for the immediate installation of these air safety bags, you are sure to save a large number of lives. But, on the down side, a few lives probably will be lost because of the accidental inflation of the bags.

A utilitarian would ask: What is the greatest good for the greatest number?

What would be your course of action?

4. Schedule vs. Budget

As the manager of a schedule-driven project, you now realize that it will be almost impossible to achieve the completion date agreed upon in the contract, which is fixed-price. There is one possible solution: put several of your project staff on overtime for the last six weeks of the project. But this additional expense will consume all of the project fee and result in a cost overrun.

* * * *

This is the classical dilemma of schedule versus budget. Most project leaders have been faced with it sometime in their careers.

As the project leader, you are concerned about satisfying two parties: your client and your upper management. Your client is insisting that the project be completed on schedule, and your upper management expects you to stay within budget. You cannot do both.

A major problem here is that the one solution that will satisfy your client will cost your company money. To complete the project on schedule, you can put several of your people on overtime, but this will cost you 1½ times their regular salaries. This additional expense will cause a cost overrun.

It is essential that you involve your manager in the decision, and go to the meeting with sufficient data that will aid the decision-making process.

What would be your course of action?

5. Schedule vs. Health & Safety

As manager of production in a manufacturing plant, you have promised your best customer that a large order of parts would be ready for shipment by a certain date. Making schedule is much more important than minimizing costs, so you have had people on overtime for the past three months. But you are now faced with a dilemma: several accidents have occurred during the past week — with the apparent cause being *worker fatigue.*

* * * *

You are in a trying situation. You have a commitment to both your customer and your people. How do you satisfy both?

Because your customer needs the parts to produce a military system on schedule — *with an absolute due date* — you have zero flexibility on schedule. The daily phone call that you receive from your customer — "Just checking on schedule" — serves as a constant reminder.

Certainly, you have a commitment to your people. Their health and safety are paramount. And when you see the unfavorable accident reports and observe your people in a state of fatigue, you know that you must take immediate action.

This situation calls for a high level of creativity in generating alternative solutions that will help you satisfy the needs of both your customer and your people.

What would be your course of action?

6. Budget vs. Health & Safety

As president of an aircraft manufacturing company, you have been informed that a highly reliable warning system for detecting approaching aircraft will soon be available. The problem: if you take the initiative in installing these devices in your planes, you will price yourself out of the market.

* * * *

You are faced with a real dilemma: between the possibility of saving human lives and the possibility of losing money for your company.

The warning system for detecting approaching aircraft has been under development for a number of years. The company has invested large amounts of money in R&D, engineering, and now, manufacturing. To assure a reasonable return on investment, the company has obtained exclusive patent rights on the new product and is now ready to market it at a hefty price.

Being completely committed to aircraft safety, you are eager to purchase the new safety devices in large numbers and have them installed immediately in all of your planes. But if yours is the only company taking the initiative in purchasing these new safety devices—which are not required by FAA—you may be placed in an adverse position on costs and prices.

How would you resolve this dilemma?

ORGANIZATIONAL DILEMMAS

Every organization has at least four different stakeholders. These are the parties who have a vested interest in the success of the enterprise: customers, employees, owners, and the general community. What are the interests and expectations of these different stakeholders?

The customers are concerned about your product or service. They are concerned about quality, price, timeliness, and availability of your product or service.

The employees are concerned about their jobs and their careers. They want fair wages, job security, good working conditions, and opportunities for advancement.

The owners are concerned about their investment. They want a reasonable financial return on their investment and an assurance that their investment is secure.

The members of the community expect your enterprise to be a "good citizen." Specifically, they expect you to provide stable employment, pay your taxes, and not pollute the environment.

These are reasonable expectations, but we can anticipate innumerable conflicts. As indicated in Figure 7, these are some of the possible conflicts: customers vs. employees, customers vs. owners, customers vs. community, employees vs. owners, employees vs. community, and owners vs. community. We will consider each.

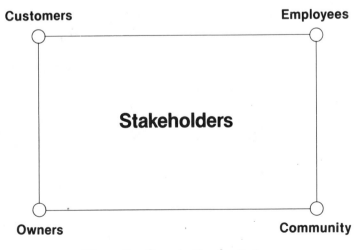

Figure 7. Organizational criteria.

1. Customers vs. Employees

As a general manager, you promised your employees a "substantial" pay raise once things turned around. They have now turned around. With inflation running at 5 percent per annum, your people are thinking in terms of at least a 10 percent pay raise just to "catch up." You will have to raise your prices a corresponding amount, and you are in a highly competitive market.

* * * *

Your people deserve the credit for the turn-around. During the past 24 months, they have worked very hard and very smart. Diligence has been the catch-word. And the reason for the two-year freeze on salary increases apparently was accepted by most of the employees. The attitude of the entire work force was: "We are all in this together, and we are going to make it work." Certainly, all of the employees should be commended for their efforts and the resulting success of their efforts.

But now it is time to "pay the piper." You made a promise of a substantial pay increase when things turned around. And, clearly, they have turned around.

Fulfilling this promise will create a serious problem: a 10 percent across-the-board pay increase would call for a corresponding increase in your prices. And your competitors have not — and probably will not — post similar increases.

The principal lesson in this case is that managers should be very careful when it comes to making promises.

What would be your course of action?

2. Customers vs. Owners

Based on all the evidence presented, you — the vice president of marketing — are now convinced that your company has distributed and sold a substandard product. In quantitative terms, it is about 20 percent lower quality than what you had advertised. If you give rebates to all of these customers, it will wipe out your entire profit margin for the year.

* * * *

Your company has been in existence for more than 100 years. During this period of time, it has achieved an excellent reputation for quality and integrity and the ensuing feeling of trust and loyalty on the part of your customers.

What caused the problem here was that the test results on the new run of products were delayed by 30 days. Your marketing people, assuming that the test results would be similar to those of previous tests, proceeded to sell the product. Now, to your surprise, the test results reveal a 20 percent lower quality than expected — and publicized in printed brochures.

We can assume that most customers will not become aware of the discrepancy between what was advertised and what they purchased. But some of your more sophisticated and knowledgeable customers are very likely to become aware of the discrepancy.

An across-the-board call-back of the product will lead to a very poor year financially. But to say nothing will lead to a very poor year ethically.

What would be your course of action?

3. Customers vs. Community

As a plant manager, you have just learned that you can offload one of your products for manufacture in Taiwan. Even including shipping costs, the cost of manufacture will be reduced by 25 percent. But this means that there will be 100 fewer jobs open to members of the local community, which has been a loyal supporter of your plant for the past 20 years.

* * * *

For the past 20 years, you have enjoyed the support of your community. Its leaders are fully aware that this is a reciprocal relationship: they help you and you help them. This is a win-win relationship in the best sense of the term — and you would like to see it continue.

But now there is a new twist. A recent financial analysis has revealed that outsourcing one of your major products for manufacture in Taiwan will result in a considerable cost savings. Specifically, you will be able to manufacture the product at a 25 percent lower cost — including shipping costs. This lower cost translates into a significant price reduction for your customers.

On the flip side of the coin, the elimination of 100 jobs would be a blow to the community. In a town with only 20,000 people, losing 100 jobs is not "small potatoes."

Here you must weigh your commitment to your customers (who are nationwide) versus your commitment to the local community.

How would you resolve this dilemma?

4. Employees vs. Owners

As a general manager, you have just been notified that one of your major projects has been unexpectedly canceled. This means that you now have 25 "surplus" employees. Based on anticipated future work load, there is a reasonably high probability that you will need all of these employees in 3–6 months. But what will you do in the meantime?

* * * *

Managers in project-oriented companies are faced with a common problem: they often have either too much work or not enough work. It is difficult to maintain a stable work load. And the unexpected cancellation of a major project will throw a monkey wrench into the best-laid plans.

In this most recent cancellation of a government-sponsored project, you now find yourself with 25 surplus employees (out of a total of 250). Without this project, the only place to charge the time of these employees is to an overhead account number. Carrying this number of people on overhead for three to six months (until a replacement project is obtained) will wipe out a big part of your projected profit for the year.

It appears that you are in a no-win situation. If you lay off the 25 surplus staff, you will be viewed as an inhumane employer by the persons terminated as well as by the remaining employees. But if you carry them on overhead, you will be viewed by the owners as a "country club" manager.

What would be your plan of action?

5. Employees vs. Community

Even though you are in a highly depressed geographical area, this has been a very profitable year for your enterprise. As a reward for great effort and productivity, you would like to give your entire work force an average pay increase of 10 percent. But most other organizations in the community are giving either minimum pay raises (2–3 percent) or, in many cases, no raises at all.

* * * *

Most managers today realize that, to achieve long-term success, they must operate as a partner in the local community. The company cannot be aloof to the local community: it cannot be "a city on the hill." When the company and the local community operate as partners, we find a relation that is mutually beneficial.

This being said, you now find yourself in a difficult situation. As the president of a medium-sized company, you are faced with a dilemma. The good news is that this has been a very profitable year for your company and you can justifiably give your people a 10 percent across-the-board pay raise. But the bad news is that some of the leaders in the community have gotten wind of this possibility and are now trying to dissuade you from taking such action. Inasmuch as the other workers in the community are expecting no more than a 2–3 percent increase, your action would create a morale problem for the "have-nots."

Certainly, you have an obligation to reward your employees fairly. And, too, you have an obligation to be responsive to the concerns expressed by the community leaders. Is there a way out?

What is the way out?

6. Owners vs. Community

As a plant manager who has studied the facts, you now believe that you have a social obligation to the local community to install a pollution control system in your plant. This will be a very costly investment. And if yours is the only plant to take such action, you will not be competitive price-wise, because your competitors in the community have not installed such systems.

* * * *

We can assume that you are a conscientious, well-intentioned plant manager. And we also can assume that you are concerned about people as well as profitability.

On the people side, it is now clear to you that your plant is generating pollution beyond acceptable levels. Your chemists have been monitoring the situation closely for several months and have presented you the irrefutable facts. Your plant is exceeding tolerable levels — but so are several other plants in the immediate vicinity. Two of these plants are your direct competitors. These are the facts, and they cannot be ignored.

On the profitability side, we are talking about a large amount of money to acquire and install a modern pollution control system. And even with a 10-year amortization period and a reasonable tax break, this investment will cut heavily into this year's profits. And if your competitors do not do likewise, you will be placed in an adverse position with respect to the pricing of your products.

What would be your plan of action?

SOCIETAL DILEMMAS

The relations between organizations and the larger society of which they are a part are interdependent. Organizations could not survive without society, and society could not survive without organizations.

There are some management theorists who contend that the organization's principal reason for existence is to serve the needs of society. Be it a school system, a hospital, or a business enterprise, the ultimate purpose of the organization is to serve society. And to the extent that the organization meets these needs, it will be successful.

Society has certain expectations of those organizations that provide goods and services. These expectations pertain to quality, price, availability, and health and safety. Members of society expect *quality* — a product or service that meets their requirements. They expect to obtain this product or service at a reasonable *price* — they do not want to be gouged. They expect it to be *available* — obtainable when they need it. And they expect it to be *safe and not injurious to their health.*

These are reasonable expectations. But, once again, we can foresee a number of potential conflicts. As suggested by the criteria shown in Figure 8, these are some of the possible conflicts: quality vs. price, quality vs. availability, quality vs. health & safety, price vs. availability, price vs. health & safety, and availability vs. health & safety. We will examine each.

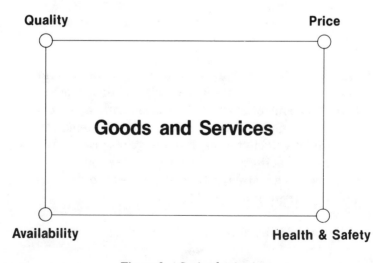

Figure 8.   Societal criteria.

1. Quality vs. Price

As a parent of four young children, you moved into your community primarily because of the excellent reputation of the public schools. And you are convinced that the schools do indeed have a quality educational program. But now the school system is asking for the support of a fourth tax levy in five years — to maintain quality. On a $100,000 home, this new levy translates into $300 per year in additional taxes. Would you support the tax levy?

* * * *

Certainly, you want a quality educational program for your children. What could be more important?

You have supported the three tax levies that were on the ballot over the last five years. Each time, the school administrators and board members said that the additional funds were needed to maintain a quality educational program. First, there was the need for the revamping of the curriculum. Next, there was a need for a computer literacy program and improved instructional technology. Then, only a year ago, there was the need for better pay and benefits for teachers. It seems that the needs of the school system are never-ending.

And now the schools are asking members of the community to support another levy — again, to maintain a quality educational program. This means another $25 per month will be added to your real estate taxes. And with your modest income, this is no trivial amount.

Are you willing to pay this additional amount to help maintain quality in your schools?

2. Quality vs. Availablility

You live in a small rural community that has no medical specialists and only three general practitioners (whose ages are 65, 70, and 72). The closest specialists are in a city 100 miles away. Of your four children, two are sickly. One is afflicted with asthma and the other has an unrelenting allergy. Both will need medical attention over the next several years. Where would you take these two children for medical care?

* * * *

Certainly, you are concerned about the health of all four of your children. But you and your spouse are especially concerned about Beatrice, who has asthma, and Benjamin, who has a serious allergy.

Because you are taking at least one of your children to a doctor every week, the availability of medical service is most important. And inasmuch as both you and your spouse have full-time jobs, getting your children to a doctor during the normal work week can be a problem.

You have gotten to know the three general practitioners in your community. Coincidentally — and perhaps unfortunately — all three of these doctors are approaching retirement. And while all three have the necessary credentials and experience to treat your children, they give you the impression that they may not be really up to date on current developments in medicine — especially those pertaining to asthma and allergies.

The specialists that could give you and your spouse the added confidence are a four-hour round trip from your home.

What would be your decision?

3. Quality vs. Health & Safety

Your 10-year-old child has contracted a rare type of cancer and is not responding to treatment. For the past six months, this has been the foremost concern in the lives of you and your spouse. You have just learned through the underground that the most potent drug for arresting the cancer is available in a clinic in Mexico City. Because the drug has not been sufficiently tested for deleterious side effects, the U. S. government has not allowed it to be marketed in this country. What would you do?

* * * *

This is something that you had read about but never believed it could happen to one of your own children. A low probability event is now at your doorstep. This problem has become the number one concern in your life. You are completely absorbed with the problem; it is difficult to think about anything else.

As a successful manager, you have been able to find a solution to every problem. That is what you were paid to do. So there must be a solution to this problem.

Your source of information regarding the drug is very reliable. But you have been alerted by your family physician that the medical community knows virtually nothing about possible adverse side effects of the drug.

Thus, the decision is in your hands. Would you take your child to Mexico City?

4. Price vs. Availability

You are a resident of a small community that has only one medical center (and the nearest hospital is 60 miles away). For a number of years the center has been open from 6:00 a.m. to 6:00 p.m. daily. The Citizens Advisory Group, of which you are the leader, has requested that the center be open 24 hours per day. The center director has said "fine" to the request, but because of the low demand during the evening hours, the cost per patient would have to be increased 25 percent. Would you still support the around-the-clock hours?

* * * *

The Citizens Advisory Group for Medical Care was formed one year ago to study the medical needs of the community and come up with a set of recommendations. You were selected to be the leader of the group.

To develop an empirically-based set of recommendations, you have conducted a comprehensive survey of the medical needs of the community. The survey revealed that the principal needs not being met were the emergencies that occurred during the time between 6:00 p.m. and 6:00 a.m.

It is true that a general hospital is only one hour away. During the past year, however, this distance to be covered has led to a number of "close calls"— at least two being almost fatal. Clearly, most people in the community would be much more at ease if the center were open 24 hours every day. But is this "peace of mind" worth an additional cost of 25 percent per case?

As the leader of the advisory group, what would be your recommendation?

5. Price vs. Health & Safety

You have two teenage daughters who are driving their own cars. Naturally, you are concerned about their safety. You have just learned that air safety bags are now available and could be installed in both cars. The cost per car would be $500. Would you make the purchase?

* * * *

Your daughter Julie is 19 and has been driving for three years. Her younger sister Jill is 17 and has been driving for only one year. As a middle-income parent, you were able to save enough money to buy each daughter a used car (as a reward for being inducted into the National Honor Society).

As a conscientious parent, you have consistently impressed upon your daughters the importance of safe driving. "Be sure to fasten your seat belt" and "drive carefully" are admonitions that still echo in their ears.

You have now reviewed the report on air safety bags in the latest *Consumers Guide.* The report presents a compelling message: air safety bags provide considerably more protection than safety belts — showing a comparative survival ratio of two to one. The facts are in.

In consideration of the evidence, would you be willing to invest $500 for the purchase of an air safety bag for each of your daughters' cars?

6. Availability vs. Health & Safety

Assume that you are a manager who travels by air at least twice every month. You have a choice between two airports: a small airport that is only a 10-minute drive from your home and a large international airport that is a 90-minute drive. The dilemma: on a recent safety evaluation of airports, the large international airport received a "9" (on a 10-point scale) and the small airport received only a "5." Assuming that you can get the proper plane connections out of either airport, which one would you choose?

* * * *

As a frequent flier, you were interested in the recent report that presented the safety evaluation scores for every commercial airport in your state. And you were especially interested in the scores achieved by the two airports that you use most frequently.

The evaluations were done by experts and appear to be objective. A quick study of the tabular data allow the reader to see, first, the scores given to each airport on each of 20 relevant factors and, then, a composite safety evaluation score.

The composite score of "9" for the large international airport gives you a feeling of confidence. But the score of only "5" for the smaller airport gives you reason for concern.

Is this difference in safety scores enough to override the inconvenience of driving the longer distance to the larger airport?

PERSONAL DILEMMAS

The individual's internal conflict in values can be illustrated through examples of conflict between needs. A need signifies a discrepancy between what the individual *has* and what he or she *desires*. The individual is "driven" or "motivated" to reduce or eliminate the discrepancy. If there is no discrepancy between what exists and what is desired, there is no motivation.

Abraham Maslow postulated that there are basic needs common to all of humankind and that these needs are arranged in a hierarchical order.[81] Moving from the bottom of the hierarchy to the top, we find these human needs:

1. **Physiological needs:** need for oxygen, water, food, rest.
2. **Security needs:** need for stability, dependency, protection, structure, law, limits.
3. **Belongingness needs:** need for affectionate relations with other people, need for a place in one's group or family.
4. **Self-esteem needs:** need for self-respect and for the esteem of others.
5. **Self-actualization needs:** need for self-fulfillment, to become all that one is capable of becoming.

As people try to satisfy specific needs, there will be some conflicts between needs. Figure 9 shows some potential conflicts: physiological needs vs. security needs, physiological needs vs. belongingness needs, physiological needs vs. self-esteem needs, security needs vs. belongingness needs, security needs vs. self-esteem needs, and belongingness needs vs. self-esteem needs. We will examine each in turn.

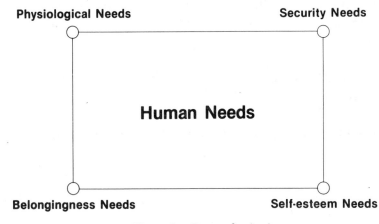

Figure 9.   Personal criteria.

1. Physiological Needs vs. Security Needs

As a 55-year-old project leader, you have been working 12 hours per day, seven days per week, for the past
two months. Your general manager expects you and
your team to continue at this pace for at least eight
more weeks in order to complete a very important
project. You now feel that this work load is taking its
toll on your health. What would you do?

* * * *

Everyone knows that you are a dedicated project
leader who would like to make a significant contribution to the success of this project. The project is important to the company, to your manager, and to you.
But in order to complete the project on schedule, it
will take a commitment from you far beyond the call
of duty. You already have made such a commitment
over the past eight weeks and are now expected to
maintain the same level of commitment over the next
eight weeks.

Through the years, you have had a reputation for
always "coming through." Despite heavy odds, you
could always "pull a project out of the fire"— to the
satisfaction of your clients as well as your own
management.

But now the situation is different. You are not as young
as you once were! And your health has not been up
to par. Certainly, you would like to see the project
completed on schedule. But at what cost? At this time,
which should have higher priority: your health or the
project?

2. Physiological Needs vs. Belongingness Needs

The only time that you and your associates at work get together socially is during lunchtime, at which time you enjoy a brown bag lunch and a game of hearts. The problem is that two of the members smoke and you do not, and the place of congregating is a small room with barely adequate ventilation. This room was chosen because company policy prohibits smoking in the offices and the cafeteria. What would you do?

* * * *

The lunchtime break is an important event in your daily life. You work a fast-paced eight or nine hours every day and are usually working under tight deadlines and considerable pressure. There is seldom an opportunity to take a break for even a few minutes during the regular working hours.

Thus, you look forward each day to the lunchtime break, which gives you an opportunity to relax and to store up sufficient energy to take on the challenges of the afternoon. And the four people you meet with daily are very fine persons. They are friendly, sociable, and follow an unwritten rule of no "job talk" during the lunch hour. This is strictly a social gathering.

But now the smoke from the cigarettes is beginning to "get to you." After an hour in this smoke-filled room, you sometimes return to your office with blood-shot eyes. As an ex-smoker, you are sympathetic toward the needs of the smokers, who have no convenient place to smoke other than this room. How would you deal with this problem?

3. Physiological Needs vs. Self-esteem Needs

Assume that you are a 200-pound man with a serious back problem. You work in an office with two small men and four average-size women. The office is located in the basement of a refurbished building. Because of the heavy rains over the past several days, the water has now backed up onto the office floor. There is an urgent need for everyone present to grab a bucket and start bailing water with great vigor. Your associates are unaware of your back condition. What would you do?

* * * *

The unrelenting rains have created a serious problem. You and your associates arrive at work at around 8:00 a.m. only to find about six inches of water on the office floor, and the water is rising rapidly. The files that contain all of the valuable documents are vulnerable: within a matter of two or three hours, many of the documents could be ruined — not to mention the new furnishings. Because of your geographical location, there is no outside help readily available. The only good news is that there are seven large metal containers that could be used to scoop out the water.

If you join the group and begin bailing the water, there is a reasonably high probability that this physical exertion will exacerbate your back condition — and may require several weeks of recovery. But if you try to bow out now with an explanation about your back problem, will your associates even believe you?

What an embarrassing situation! Something that you had never anticipated. You are truly in a predicament, and a decision must be made immediately.

What would you do?

4. Security Needs vs. Belongingness Needs

Assume that you are a foreman in a factory and have developed a close relationship with your co-workers. You have a plant manager who seems to distrust everyone. He is now taking a one-week vacation and just before he departed last Friday, instructed you to report to him the time of arrival and time of departure of each foreman on the day shift. For the past two days, three of these foremen have deviated from the 7:00 to 4:00 rule. (Alert: it is possible that the foreman has someone checking on you.) What would you do?

* * * *

Theory X managers still may be found in some quarters. As a part of his Theory X personality syndrome, your general manager has a touch of paranoia. He has a deep suspicion that most of his foremen are trying to make him look bad. To counteract this subterfuge, he employs elaborate schemes to have one foreman check on the activities of another foreman and then solicit a third to check on the first. And so it goes in a maze of plotting and counter-plotting.

Your general manager has now placed you in an untenable position. If you prize only your job security and become a "squealer" on your co-workers, you are certain to be ostracized by them. But if you prize only your acceptance by your co-workers and ignore any deviations on their part, you may be placing your job in jeopardy.

Because of the job market at this particular time and in this particular location, you would find it very difficult to find another job with equal pay and benefits.

Where would you place your primary loyalty? What would your actions be?

5. Security Needs vs. Self-esteem Needs

As a research scientist in a contract research organization, you have been heavily involved for several weeks
in a preparing a research proposal that is to be submitted to an outside client. This is certain to be an
excellent technical proposal, but the competition will
be tough, and winning the project will depend on your
organization having the exact equipment needed to
carry out the research. Your organization does not
presently have all of the equipment but plans to obtain it if the competition is won. Your manager wants
you to modify the written proposal to imply that all
of the needed equipment is now in place. What would
you do?

* * * *

You have every right to be proud of your proposal. The
document in its present form reflects an excellent grasp
of the subject, has a very sound plan of action, and
is well organized and well written. The three technical
reviewers have applauded your proposal.

Your department manager has now reviewed the proposal and comes to your office with the proposal in
hand. This is what he says: "I think that you have an
excellent technical proposal. It is very sound. But I
want you to make one minor change before it is submitted. Where you state we will purchase the remaining equipment if we are awarded the contract, I want
you to change the wording to imply that all of the
equipment is now in place. This slight modification
should increase our odds of winning the contract. . . .
And don't be concerned, because all of our competitors
do the same thing."

After making certain that you understood his instructions, what would be your reply?

6. Belonginess Needs vs. Self-esteem Needs

You are in a meeting with the other four members of a project team. The five of you are energetically discussing an issue that is critical to the project's success. It is now obvious that your four associates are in unanimous agreement on the issue. But you are 180° off from where they are. They now ask you to present your views on the matter. What would you say?

* * * *

Everyone should be able to relate to this situation. Something akin to what is presented here occurs again and again — whenever several people are working together in an attempt to arrive at an agreed upon solution to a common problem.

In a nutshell, should you be other-directed or inner-directed? If you opt to be other-directed, you will go along with the majority. But if you opt to be inner-directed, you will express your own views on the matter.

Going along with the majority has the possible advantage of promoting harmony and your being viewed as a good team player. But on the negative side, the team may lose a good idea and you may not feel very good about yourself afterwards.

Expressing your views on the matter has the advantage of possibly adding a worthwhile idea for consideration and enhancing your own self-esteem. But on the negative side, it may cause disruption and argumentation (depending, of course, on the personalities of the team members).

What would you do?

SUMMING UP

In dealing with conflict in values, the manager must beware of rationalization. This is a subject that Barbara Ley Toffler makes special note of in her book *Tough Choices*. She highlights the seriousness of the problem:

> When we rationalize a decision we have made, or an action we have taken, we give creditable, although often untrue, reasons for why we have done as we have done. It is an instinctive response driven by a need for psychological self-protection, and no amount of admonition to beware of its effects on the management of ethical dilemmas is likely to abolish it. However, any manager seeking to contribute to creating an ethically responsible organization must be aware of the instinct to rationalize, and must, if not control it, recognize it and recognize the realities it is masking.[119, p.344]

Four commonly held rationalizations that can lead to misconduct on the part of managers have been delineated by Saul Gellerman:
- A belief that the activity is within reasonable ethical and legal limits — that is, that it is not "really" illegal or immoral.
- A belief that the activity is in the individual's or the corporation's best interests — that the individual would somehow be expected to undertake the activity.
- A belief that the activity is "safe" because it will never be found out or publicized; the classic crime-and-punishment issue of discovery.
- A belief that because the activity helps the company, the company will condone it and even protect the person who engages in it.[43]

These observations lead to a clear message for all managers: *Don't get caught in the rationalization trap.* And heed the words of Toffler when she says:

> Rationalizing denies the organization the opportunity to understand its mistakes and to increase its capabilities for ethical management. In sum, rationalization's greatest sin is not that it encourages individual self-delusion, but that it promotes the organizational status quo.[119, p.345]

* * * *

We stated at the outset that managers frequently are faced with ethical dilemmas and that these dilemmas result from a conflict of values. A value has been defined as a guiding principle for our everyday lives. Whenever we are confronted with a situation that involves two or more values that cannot be satisfied simultaneously, we have a conflict in values.

A common conflict facing the manager is choosing between a *right* decision and a *good* decision. *Right* and *wrong* refer to the ethical dimension, and good and bad refer to the economic dimension. The effective leader-manager will strive to make right-good decisions.

To achieve success in making right-good decisions, the leader-manager must be cognizant of four particular spheres of concern and the criteria associated with each of these spheres:

- **End results** (quality, schedule, budget, health & safety)
- **The organization** (customers, employees, owners, community)
- **The society** (quality, price, availability, health & safety)
- **The individual** (physiological needs, security needs, belongingness needs, self-esteem needs)

To illustrate conflict in values, we have presented examples of dilemmas in each of these four spheres. But these 24 examples merely "scratch the surface." A more thorough delineation of possible conflicts could fill a large book.

In sum, this chapter illustrates the real world of managerial decision making. The issues are complex and there are few cookbook answers.

Regarding the reality of managerial decision making, I am reminded of a one-liner by the comedian Lily Tomlin who was bemoaning the plight of the street people. Playing the role of a bag lady, she remarked, "Our only problem is coping with reality." And so it is.

Day in and day out, managers must cope with reality. And a significant part of this reality is the ability to cope with ethical dilemmas. To this end, managers need a framework for making ethical decisions, a framework that provides both a sound philosophical base and practical guidelines for action. It is the philosophical base to which we now turn.

III

The Good Life

No limits are set to the ascent of man, and to each and
everyone the highest stands open. Here it is only your personal choice that decides.

Martin Buber
Ten Rungs[25, p.71]

*Introduction • Empirical Existence • Consciousness at Large • Spirit •
Existenz • Reason • Summing Up*

INTRODUCTION

Socrates noted that the question of ethics was how we should live.
It is the quest for, and the understanding of, the good life, a life worth
living. It is possible to use the word "ethical" of any design for living
that would provide a reasonable answer to Socrates' question.

"Once the question is constituted that way," says Bernard
Williams, "it very naturally moves from the question, asked by
anybody, 'how should I live?' to the question 'how should anybody
live?' That seems to ask for the reasons we all share for living in one
way rather than another. It seems to ask for the conditions of the
good life — the right life, perhaps, for human beings as such."[127, p.20]

Assuming, then, that the question of ethics is that of the good
life, the question then becomes: What particular model of human
nature will aid us in our quest? We need a model that is sufficiently
comprehensive to capture human nature in its richness and diver-

69

sity and that will include both the "highs" and "lows" of human nature. We need a model that is sufficiently comprehensive to capture human beings in their totality, including both their inner selves and their outer selves. A partial model will not suffice; we need a holistic model.

Karl Jaspers, the renowned German philosopher, provides us with a useful paradigm of human nature in his idea of the "Encompassing." Jaspers first presented the idea of the "Encompassing" in a series of lectures in 1935, which were subsequently published in the book *Reason and Existenz.*[59] For the next 30 years or so, this basic notion served as the cornerstone for his philosophizing. It is as though Jaspers' conceptual framework of human nature had been "waiting in the wings"—waiting to be applied to the field of ethics.

In presenting the idea of the Encompassing, Jaspers acknowledges that he is not the originator of the specific concepts included in the general model. These have been formulated by the great philosophers over the ages. What Jaspers contributes is the integration of the specific ideas into a comprehensive framework.

The essence of the Encompassing is articulated by an American philosopher/essayist whom Jaspers admired. In the words of Ralph Waldo Emerson:

> We are taught by great actions that the universe is the property of every individual in it. Every rational creature has all nature for his dowry and estate. It is his, if he will. He may divest himself of it; he may creep into a corner, and abdicate his kingdom, as most men do, but he is entitled to the world by his constitution. In proportion to the energy of his thought and will, he takes up the world unto himself.[36] p.16

What Emerson is saying is that there is a rich world waiting out there to be *encompassed* by each human being. What part and how much of that world are to be brought within oneself is up to each person, because it will not enter automatically. And this decision has momentous consequences: on the ladder of human development, it will determine what each person is to become. Each of us has the choice of either remaining on a lower rung or continuing to move up the ladder. Stated another way, we can say that each person has the choice of being either a partially functioning human being or a fully functioning human being.

According to Jaspers, the Encompassing includes four modes of being:

- **Empirical existence** — living in the everyday world, seeking pleasure and avoiding pain.
- **Consciousness at large** — acquisition of objective knowledge, universally valid knowledge, that which is common to all.
- **Spirit** — identification with the leading ideas of movements, parties, institutions, or organizations.
- **Existenz** — achievement of authentic selfhood.[59]

These modes of being may be described in terms of our internal "maps" of the world. Our maps are our bridge to the external world. They constitute our view of reality and truth.

In *The Road Less Traveled*, M. Scott Peck illuminates the role of maps in our lives:

> Our view of reality is like a map with which to negotiate the terrain of life. If the map is true and accurate, we will generally know where we are, and if we have decided on where we want to go, we will generally know how to get there. If the map is false and inaccurate, we generally will be lost.[101, p.44]

In echoing Emerson, Peck stresses that map making requires effort:

> We are not born with maps; we have to make them, and the making requires effort. The more effort we make to appreciate and perceive reality, the larger and more accurate our maps will be. But many do not want to make this effort. Their maps are small and sketchy, their views of the world narrow and misleading.[101, pp.44-45]

If individuals are willing to make the effort, they will be able to create a series of ascending maps that will help them become fully functioning human beings. At the level of empirical existence, they will be able to create maps for coping with the everyday world. At the level of consciousness at large, they will be able to create maps of objective and universally valid knowledge. At the level of spirit, they will be able to create maps of leading ideas and beliefs with which they wish to identify. And at the level of Existenz, they will become aware that they have the freedom to create their own maps. These maps then become the building blocks of each person's self-being.

With regard to the generation of maps, it is important to appreciate the distinction between *potential* Existenz and *actual* Existenz. The person who simply adopts the maps of others — without even questioning their validity — has not gone beyond the level of *potential* Existenz. But the person who, acting in freedom, takes an active part in generating his or her own maps has moved toward *actual* Existenz — that is, the state of authentic selfhood.

The person functioning at the level of actual Existenz is guided by reason, which is the bond that unites the four modes of being. Jaspers defines reason as "the total will to communication." Reason is not unity but rather the will to unity.

This will to unity, notes Jaspers, "wants to turn toward everything that is capable of expression, toward everything that is, in order to preserve it."[59, p.64] "Reason prevents us from being suffocated in a mode of the Encompassing to which we surrender ourselves completely."[60, p.182]

Jaspers stresses that the fully functioning person is never completely stuck within a single mode of being. All modes are at his or her disposal — all guided by reason.

As the individual moves from mode to mode, it is not like jumping from island to island. Rather, as shown in Figure 10, it is like climbing a ladder containing four rungs, with the rungs held firmly

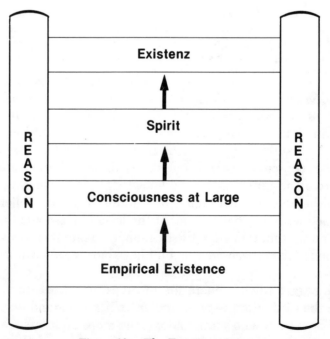

Figure 10.   The Encompassing.

in place by the two sides. The four rungs represent the four modes of being, and the two sides represent reason — the bond that connects the modes of being.

The modes of being are arranged in a hierarchical order. With empirical existence at the bottom rung of the hierarchy, we move up to consciousness at large, then to spirit, and finally to Existenz. In the self-actualizing person, each higher level includes the lower levels, but the lower levels do not include the higher levels. And importantly, the higher levels provide direction for the lower levels.

Jaspers realizes, of course, that any particular hierarchy of modes of being is subject to debate. Who is to say that one mode is at a higher position than another? By what authority can we make such a claim? It seems clear that such a position cannot be taken purely on the basis of empirical evidence. We must base our argument on reason.

In justifying the proposed hierarchy, it appears to me that this would be a logical argument:

1. The human being in a state of nature (empirical existence) is at the bottom rung of the ladder that is intended to represent the fully functioning person.
2. The human being who has acquired a great deal of objective knowledge (consciousness at large) is at a higher level than the human being in a state of nature.
3. The human being who has adopted a coherent set of ideas to provide direction for his or her life (spirit) is at a higher level than the one who has merely acquired a repository of information.
4. The human being who has achieved authentic selfhood through freedom of thought (Existenz) is at a higher level than the one who has merely adopted the ideas and beliefs of a given society, institution, or organization.

This argument undoubtedly would have little meaning to those individuals who are completely stuck at a lower rung in the hierarchy. But to those individuals who have worked their way up to the level of Existenz (namely, those persons who think philosophically), the argument should be persuasive.

"Life must be lived on a higher plane," says Emerson. "We must go up to a higher platform, to which we are always invited to ascend; there, the whole aspect of things changes."[36, p.601]

Given this rationale to justify the hierarchy, we are then in a better position to distinguish between *potential Existenz* and Existenz. The individual in a state of potential Existenz resides on some lower rung of the ladder, whereas the person who has achieved Existenz resides on the top rung. The latter person "lives out of the Encompassing" and is considered to be a "fully functioning person."

In sum, we are proposing that Jaspers' paradigm of human nature — the Encompassing — provides a reasonable answer to Socrates' question of how one should live. Granted, the paradigm does not furnish a detailed prescription for living, but it does provide a meaningful framework for living. It is then the responsibility of each individual to embellish the framework through his or her own experiences and beliefs.

The Encompassing may be viewed as an integrative ethical theory that can accommodate the more focused ethical systems of Mill, Kant, Rousseau, and Buber. We will show how each of these schools of thought is part of a larger whole, and when integrated within the Encompassing, can provide the leader-manager with a decision making framework.

But before examining these various ethical systems, we will elaborate on the nature of the four modes of being and reason. This elaboration should give greater clarity to the meaning of the Encompassing, which will serve as the theoretical base for all that is to follow.

EMPIRICAL EXISTENCE

The bottom rung of the ladder — empirical existence — is the first of the four modes of being. What does "the good life" mean to a person who lives exclusively in this mode of being?

In the book *Karl Jaspers: An Introduction to His Philosophy*, Charles Wallraff presents a succinct description of empirical existence:

> Empirical existence may be viewed as virtually identical with Hobbes's man in a state of nature: a practicing hedonist entirely devoid of other-regarding impulses and concerned only to preserve and enhance his own being. For such a man, desire and aversion are the guides of life, and nothing can be good or bad apart from them.[122, p.200]

This is the individual who is "looking out for number one." As an egoist, this person believes that the world is designed to meet his or her particular needs. Individual self-interest is the actual motive of all conscious action. Seeking pleasure and avoiding pain are the principal guides of life, and any notion of right and wrong is limited to these two aims.

According to Jaspers, empirical existence has these salient features:

- The human being is viewed as an object — determined by the external forces of the world and susceptible to being investigated scientifically.
- Life has a beginning and end in objective time.
- Human existence is fleeting temporal existence.
- The purpose of life is to preserve one's own physical being.
- The driving force in life is impulse, desire, the search for happiness.
- Happiness consists in simply existing.
- There is a self-dissolving pseudo-identity with events of the moment.
- Human potentiality has no meaning beyond human actuality: the "is" and the "ought" are synonymous.
- The empirical average is viewed as "normal" and "right."
- It is an unexamined life.

Implicit in these features is a set of poorly framed values. My views of the values that serve as the guiding principles for an individual living exclusively in the mode of empirical existence are presented in Figure 11. They are elaborated below.

Pleasure: If it feels good, "go for it."

Absence of pain: Take precautions to avoid anything that might cause discomfort to you.

Self-gratification: Enjoy life to the fullest, for tomorrow you will be dead.

Self-preservation: Avoid commitment and protect yourself from being hurt.

Security: Be sure that you have the "most toys" of any kid on the block.

Utility: Assign value to everything on the basis of how well it helps you achieve pleasure and avoid pain.

Practicality: Focus only on that which relates to the sensory life; everything else is academic.

Figure 11.   Values associated with empirical existence.

Acquisitiveness: Obtain the material possessions that will give you self-gratification and security.

Maneuverability: Never allow yourself to get "boxed into a corner"; make certain that there is always an "out."

Power: Establish the wherewithal to control others and resist being controlled by others.

To see how these values associated with empirical existence apply in the everyday world, we now consider the life of a person who lives by them. To the question—"What is your philosophy of life?"— this was the response given by Chris:

"Well, frankly, I have difficulty with your question. I have never really given any thought to my philosophy of life. Philosophy is a subject that has always seemed very abstract to me. It has no relevance to the real world. But I can tell you what's important to me. I can tell you what I believe about the meaning of life.

"First and foremost, I believe in looking out for number one. If I don't look out for myself, no one else will.

"My primary goal in life is to get as much enjoyment as I possibly can. There is so much out there to enjoy — and I want it all. Anything that prevents me from satisfying my desire for pleasure is an obstacle. And anything that helps me satisfy my desire for pleasure is a useful resource.

"I believe in the old adage, 'Live for today, for tomorrow you may be dead'. Who knows, I could be killed by a train tomorrow. Or I might be inflicted with cancer. I am going to make the most of it while I can.

"I believe that the end justifies the means. The end that I am always working toward is to maximize pleasure and avoid pain. Anything that will help me achieve this goal is good, and anything that will prevent me from achieving this goal is bad. Winning is everything! It's all quite simple.

"This leads me to the subject of ethics. I look at ethics in terms of right and wrong. What is right is whatever helps me achieve my goal. What is wrong is whatever prevents me from achieving my goal. Furthermore, I believe that ethics is relative — you know, 'When in Rome, do as the Romans do'. There are no absolutes.

"With regard to friends, these are people I can use to achieve my own ends. And there's nothing really wrong with this, because this is how my so-called friends use me. As we always say, 'You scratch my back, and I'll scratch yours'.

"Then a person comes to the end of the road. I believe that when it's all over — when one approaches the end of life — the real winner is the one with the most trophies. That's what it's all about.

"You asked me earlier what I would like to have written as my epitaph. I never really thought about it before, but I think I would like to have engraved on my tombstone, 'Chris had fun while it lasted'."

This, then, describes the individual who lives exclusively on the bottom rung of the ladder — at the lowest level of personal existence. Granted, this is a hypothetical case, and is presented as a "pure type," but it nevertheless reflects the actual lives of no small number of individuals.

This brief analysis leads to a relevant question: What is the meaning of truth for a person who resides exclusively at the level of empirical existence? There is a straightforward answer: truth is found in usefulness of consequences. Truth is that which is useful to a life of pleasure; untruth is that which hinders or obstructs it. Truth is relative, alterable, and arbitrary.

In concluding this analysis of empirical existence, we should consider its limitations when viewed as the exclusive mode of existence. Wallraff makes this observation:

> When separated from the other modes, empirical existence is remarkably primitive. It suggests the cynic's idea of man, the proletariat in Orwell's 1984, or a human organism devoid of moral and religious values, as delineated by a rigorous behaviorist. [122, p.200]

CONSCIOUSNESS AT LARGE

We now move to the second rung of the ladder — consciousness at large. What does "the good life" mean to a person who lives primarily at this level of being?

Charles Wallraff captures the essence of consciousness at large:

> Plato's discussion of the line which divides sense-perception from understanding, followed by the myth of the cave which illustrates it, may be taken to signify the leap from empirical existence to consciousness at large. . . . At the level of consciousness at large the scientific understanding provides clarity and distinctness, settles opinions and puts end to doubt, and offers the sort of coercive certainty that constitutes knowledge at its best. [122, p.202]

Some readers will recall Plato's parable of the cave. The several lifelong inhabitants in that particular habitat had an extremely restricted view of reality. Because of their chains, their vision was limited to a single wall of the cave, observing day in and day out the shadows reflected by the fire. These shadows constituted reality — and their only reality. Eventually, one of the dwellers was able to escape from the confines of the cave and discovered to his amazement an entirely new world on the outside of the cave. In Plato's metaphor, the "enlightened one" moved from knowledge through sense-perception to knowledge through understanding. In the language of M. Scott Peck, the individual formed a completely new set of maps of reality. In the language of the Encompassing, the individual advanced from empirical existence to consciousness at large.

According to Jaspers, consciousness at large has these principal features:

- Consciousness at large is the locality of valid thought.
- Consciousness at large is what in our individually varied consciousness of experience and reality we call the consciousness common to all.
- Consciousness at large is the point where each can substitute for any other, a point conceived as unique and more or less shared by all.
- Consciousness at large provides clarity and distinctness, settles opinions, and puts an end to doubt.
- Consciousness at large offers the sort of coercive certainty that constitutes knowledge at its best.
- The contents of consciousness at large include both empirical facts and logical evidence.
- The contents of consciousness at large appear precisely the same to all rational creatures.
- When a person considers the Pythagorean theorem, that person knows that what is in him or her is precisely the same as what is within anyone else who is thinking that theorem.
- Consciousness at large judges, and its judgment constitutes the recognition of a universal validity.
- By virtue of consciousness at large we partake in a realm of fixed, valid meaning, and with it we reach as far as it is possible for any mode of universal validity.

Underlying these several features is a set of evolving values. My views of the values that serve as the guiding principles for an individual living primarily in the mode of consciousness at large are shown in Figure 12. They are defined below.

Certainty: free from doubt or reservation.

Fact: that which actually exists.

Objectivity: free from personal feelings or prejudice.

Evidence: that which tends to prove or disprove something.

Clarity: being free from ambiguity.

Precision: being exactly that and nothing more nor less.

Demonstrability: capable of being demonstrated conclusively.

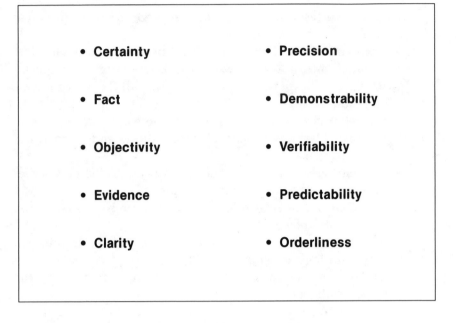

- Certainty
- Precision

- Fact
- Demonstrability

- Objectivity
- Verifiability

- Evidence
- Predictability

- Clarity
- Orderliness

Figure 12. Values associated with consciousness at large.

Verifiability: capable of being confirmed as the truth.

Predictability: capable of being foretold with precision of calculation.

Orderliness: being governed by system or method.

Given these values associated with consciousness at large, we will now consider the life of a person who lives by them. In response to the question —"What is your philosophy of life?"— this is what Marty said:

"Yes, I believe that I do have a well-thought-out philosophy of life. It includes my basic beliefs about the nature of the world, my concept of God, my life purpose, my values, and my approach to life. I believe that my philosophy would stand up to the test of internal consistency.

"First and foremost, I have a scientific orientation to life. Science provides me with a world orientation and guidance for my daily life. Science provides me with certainty; there are very few ambiguities in my life.

"Through my studies and observations, I am convinced that nature is orderly and uniform. Nature is guided by scientific laws, and these laws can be uncovered and understood. And that is my quest.

"With regard to my views on the nature of God, I believe that God is the universe; they are one and the same. In some respects, God is the Great Mystery — the part of the universe that we do not yet understand. To the extent that we understand the universe, we understand God. Thus, God is no more and no less than the universe. If you ask me if I believe in God, I can answer 'certainly'— because I believe in the universe.

"This being stated, I can say that my principal goal in life is to uncover objective truth and to live by that truth. There is only one truth, and that is objective truth, scientific truth. I have an unquenchable thirst for knowledge, that is, for objective knowledge, and I will spend my remaining days seeking that knowledge. I read, I observe, I reflect, and I continue to learn.

"With respect to my personal values, they are derived from science. These are the hallmarks of science: facts, objectivity, evidence, orderliness, and universality. These are my values; they fit me like a glove.

"Something that I learned fairly early in life is that human values can be derived completely from natural laws. We don't have to look beyond the laws of nature to arrive at a meaningful set of values to guide our lives. Consider these connections: if I am a heavy smoker, there is a reasonably high probability that I will be afflicted with lung cancer; if I drink too much at the Saturday night party, I probably will have a headache on Sunday morning; and if I engage in promiscuous sex, I may get AIDS. It's right there in the laws of nature.

"So I would say that my system of ethics revolves around the laws of nature. If I live by these laws, there will be good consequences. If I ignore the laws of nature, I will surely suffer. It's as simple and straightforward as that.

"In applying these ideas to my daily life, I have an effective strategy for coping with problems. It is grounded in the scientific method, a well tested approach for dealing with any problem. Essentially, it involves these steps: define the problem, collect the relevant facts, generate alternative solutions, evaluate the alternatives in terms of cost/benefit, select the best alternative, and then implement that alternative. This is a powerful method, and it works.

"Just to wrap up, you asked me what I would like to have written on my epitaph. Very simple. I would like for it to read, 'Marty lived by the laws of nature'."

This, then, describes the individual who lives primarily on the second rung of the ladder—at the level of consciousness at large. Anyone who is committed to a scientific orientation to life probably can relate very well to the ideas expressed here.

What is the meaning of truth for a person who resides primarily at the level of consciousness at large? The answer lies in the essence of science: truth is *cogent correctness*. It is universally valid, and any knowledgeable person will see its correctness.

Even though scientific truth is universally valid, it is not the *whole* truth. Jaspers stresses the point:

> Although consciousness at large, this realm of the sciences, is also the realm where matters become clear for us because they can be stated, yet its compelling correctness is by no means ever in itself alone the absolute truth. Rather, truth emerges from *all* modes of the Encompassing.[57, p.36]

SPIRIT

We examine next the third rung of the ladder—spirit. What does "the good life" mean to a person who resides primarily in this mode of being?

Wallraff provides us with a definition of spirit:

> Spirit is the author of "ideas." These ideas furnish a background for our thoughts and actions. We have theoretical ideas of matter, life, the soul, and God; and our behavior is guided by ideas of the physician, the university, the state, the world, and so on. They do not constitute determinate knowledge, but rather the sort of indeterminate thought that serves as an atmosphere or tacitly held frame of reference within which our thinking can proceed.[122, p.205]

The German word that Jaspers uses to communicate this third level of being is "Geist." Some American writers translate Geist into mind, whereas others translate it into spirit. Because the notion of mind is restricted to the intellect, most writers prefer spirit. Geist is more than intellect.

Most people would assume that such diverse world views as Christianity and Communism have little in common. With regard to specific content, this may be true. But with regard to the particular level of being at which these two world views are manifested, they have much in common. Both of these philosophies of life are absorbed and revealed at the level of *spirit* — the level at which we find a set of leading ideas to guide our lives.

According to Jaspers, spirit has these salient features:

- Spirit is the desire to become whole.
- This whole — itself not an object but a force that penetrates everything, attracts as goal, acts as a driving impulse within me, crystallizes into the objective forms of configuration and patterns — is called *idea*.
- The notion that spirit is idea presents me yet a new experience of existence: I am actual to the extent to which I am borne up and overpowered by ideas.
- The effective idea superimposes an invisible order on all wholeness that is merely thought.
- Spirit is that which builds up, determines criteria and aims, brings forth cohesive continuity, provides an interior bond.
- Spirit creates an atmosphere, as it were, in which something happens that cannot be sufficiently explained by the understanding.
- Spirit is active, present, effective wholeness; it is active — in thought, feeling, and deed — by holding together.
- Spirit provides structure, measure, and the setting of limits.
- Spirit is as actual as empirical existence and as inward as consciousness at large but, springing from another source, it is more than these two modes of being.
- Spirit makes no decisions but excels just as much in the service of the devil as of God.

The concept of spirit highlights the connection between the individual and society. Jaspers makes special note of the connection:

> Human beings exist only in society. It is the material premise on which every individual has come to be. Society provided him with the living conditions and with the tradition that awakened his mind and made him what he is, and it remains a condition of his existence. He would inwardly take it along even if he could isolate himself on an island.[56, p.318]

Embedded within these features is a set of values. My views of the values that serve as the guiding principles for an individual living primarily in the mode of spirit are presented in Figure 13. They are defined below.

Compelling ideas: conceptions of what is desirable or ought to be.

Coherence: being naturally or logically connected.

Wholeness: a set of ideas complete in itself.

Sharing: participating in and enjoying jointly.

Community: a social group sharing a common set of ideas.

Harmony: being in a state of mutual understanding and peaceful relationship.

Conviction: belief in the truth of the ideas of the community.

Commitment: pledging support for the ideas of the community.

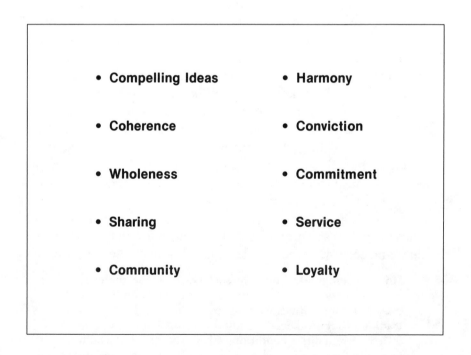

Figure 13.   Values associated with spirit.

Service: ready to be of help or use to the community.

Loyalty: faithfulness and adherence to the ideas of the community.

Given these values associated with spirit, we will now consider the life of a person who lives by them.* In response to the question — "What is your philosophy of life?"— this is what Jerry said:

"Yes, if we define 'philosophy of life' in terms of the beliefs and values that guide my life, I can agree that I do have a philosophy of life. I believe that I can summarize it in terms of a few leading ideas.

"First, I have a religious orientation to life. Religion is at the core of my being; it serves as the compass that guides my life. I am guided and propelled by faith, not by faith alone, but primarily by faith.

"Basically, I believe that God's will is revealed in the Bible, which is interpreted by the church. God is Eternal Goodness; the Bible contains the message of Eternal Goodness; and the church communicates the spirit of Eternal Goodness. God, the Bible, and the church convey a common message: 'Hold fast to the good'.

"I identify with the church. Here there is a genuine community — a group of caring people with a common mission and common values. I am part of the church, and the church is part of me. The spirit of the church has helped me become what I am. Without this involvement in the church, I would not be a complete person.

"I believe that Jesus is an ideal role model. Here was a caring person who gave unconditional love. I believe that Jesus shows the way.

"My principal goal in life is to be a good Christian. This means doing the best that I can to pattern my life after that of Jesus. From purity of heart to actual deeds, I want to live a Christian life. And I try to do this seven days a week.

"The principal value that guides my life is love. As stated in the *Epistle of John*: 'God is love, and he who abides in love abides in God and God abides in him. No man has ever seen God. If we love one another, God abides in us and his love is perfected in us'.

"Consistent with my principal value, my system of ethics is centered in the Golden Rule: 'So whatever you wish that others would do to you, do so to them'. The Golden Rule is the cornerstone of my philosophy of life.

---

*The illustration used here is Christian. But the concept of spirit could be just as readily communicated by use of any other religion (Judaism, Hinduism, Islam, etc.) or social philosophy (Confucianism, Marxism, etc.).

"I believe that the Christian message is the greatest story ever told. Here is a beautiful philosophy of life, including a life mission, a set of values, and a system of ethics. And I can learn and live this philosophy by being an active member of my church. I really couldn't ask for much more.

"You asked me what I would like to have written as my epitaph. This is what I would hope it would say: 'Jerry was a good Christian'."

This, then, describes the person who lives primarily on the third rung of the ladder — at the level of spirit. Anyone who has a religious orientation to life probably can relate very well to the ideas expressed here.

What is the meaning of truth for a person who resides primarily at the level of spirit? "It is *conviction* which counts," says Jaspers, "a conviction which is confirmed out of the idea."[59, p.83] The individual believes in the truth of the ideas of a particular community — a society, an institution, or an organization.

For some, this particular form of truth may be accepted as in itself alone the highest truth, the absolute truth. But Jaspers keeps nudging us onward — to expand our view of truth.

Jaspers warns us of the danger of being completely stuck at the level of spirit:

> For the constant threat to Existenz is that its existence may become a social existence, a static life in the order of external things; but this would turn human beings into grains of sand and rob them of their self-being.[56, p.338]

EXISTENZ

We move now to the top rung of the ladder — Existenz. What does "the good life" mean to a person who lives primarily in this mode of being?

Once again, we turn to Charles Wallraff for clarification:

> The self is more than empirical existence and consciousness at large, and it aspires to more than the pursuit of truth under the guidance of ideas. Still lacking is the moral center of the individual, viz., "Existenz." ... Nietzsche recommended through his prophet, Zarathustra, that every man be referred to himself, saying, "Now this is *my* way. Where is yours? Faithfully follow your own path; in this way you will follow me."[122, p.207, p.212]

We have now arrived at the level of being that constitutes authentic selfhood. At the level of empirical existence, the individual's identity is immersed in actions and consequences. At the level of consciousness at large, it is immersed in common understanding of objective knowledge. And at the level of spirit, it is immersed in the ideas and values of a particular community. But nowhere has the individual been revealed as a unique person, as an authentic self. In all three modes, personhood has slipped through the net. Only at the level of Existenz do we find the individual revealed as a genuine person — as an authentic self.

According to Jaspers, Existenz has these principal features:

- This Encompassing that I am and know as empirical existence, consciousness at large, and spirit, is not conceivable in itself but refers beyond itself.
- I am not only empirical existence, and am not merely consciousness at large, and am not only spirit but can, in all of these, be myself or be lost in them.
- In all modes of the Encompassing, the self can become genuinely certain of itself only as Existenz.
- Without Existenz everything seems empty, hollowed out, without ground, fake, because everything has turned into endless masks, mere possibilities, or mere empirical existence.
- Existenz is a fundamental origin, the condition of selfhood without which all the vastness of existence becomes a desert.
- Existenz is the axis about which everything in the world turns if it is to have any genuine meaning for us.
- Each Existenz is unique, unrepeatable, irreplaceable.
- Existenz is the drive to authenticity.
- Existenz is always in the process of choosing whether to be or not to be and must decide about itself.
- The central point of philosophizing is first reached in the awareness of potential Existenz.

Implicit within these various features is a set of values. My views of the values that serve as the guiding principles for a person living in the mode of Existenz are shown in Figure 14. They are defined below.

Selfhood: the state of being an individual person.

Figure 14.   Values associated with Existenz.

Independence: being an inner-directed person.

Originality: ability to express oneself in an independent and original manner.

Authenticity: congruence between the inner person and the outer person.

Communication: honest and open exchange of thoughts and feelings between two authentic selves.

Questioning: manifesting intellectual curiosity – the desire to understand and to know.

Openness: being receptive to new ideas and different points of view.

Reason: the total will to communication.

Freedom: our capacity to mold ourselves.

Responsibility: the experience of being a determinant of what happens.

Given these values associated with Existenz, we will now consider the life of a person who lives by them. In reply to the question — "What is your philosophy of life?"—this is what Jody said:

"Yes, I can answer in the affirmative that I have a philosophy of life. This is something of great importance to me, and I have devoted much time and effort to working it out. But it is by no means in a state of completion. It is still in the process of being developed, and probably always will be — for the rest of my life.

"I have a philosophical orientation to life. By that, I don't mean the study of academic philosophy. Rather, I mean a lifelong search for wisdom. Plato reminds us that philosophy is the love of wisdom rather than being in possession of wisdom. I believe that each person has the potential for being his or her own philosopher — not in the professional sense but in the everyday sense, in the way one lives his or her life.

"My 'way to wisdom' involves a threefold approach. First, I study the great teachers (including Jesus, Buddha, Confucius, Socrates, Plato, St. Augustine, and Kant). Second, I reflect on the lives and ideas of the great teachers and formulate my own ideas in the form of a unified philosophy of life. And third, I endeavor to live this philosophy on a daily basis. This is an ongoing process — one that I will pursue for the rest of my days.

"So, yes, I do have a philosophy of life. But does it represent *the* truth? No, not at all. Here I agree with the poet, Kahlil Gibran, when he says, "Say not 'I have found *the* truth', but rather, 'I have found *a* truth'." Thus, I can only say that the particular truth that I have arrived at is meaningful for me — not necessarily for others. But I do believe that the *process* I have followed in arriving at this truth could be followed by every person — at least by every person who desires to pursue philosophy as a way of life.

"Underlying my philosophy of life are three basic beliefs — regarding uniqueness, freedom, and responsibility. The three are interrelated.

"First, I believe that each person born into this world is unique. Each person has unique potentialities. And each person's foremost task is to realize these unique potentialities.

"Second, I believe in freedom of thought. Certainly important are physical freedom, political freedom, and religious freedom. But the highest freedom of all is freedom of thought — the capability to do one's own thinking.

"And third, I believe in personal responsibility. It was Ashley Montagu who suggested, 'On the east coast we have the Statue of Liberty, and on the west coast we should have the Statue of Responsibility.' And I agree that the two are inseparable.

"Given these three basic beliefs, my primary goal in life is to achieve self-actualization and to help others achieve self-actualization. To become what I am capable of becoming is my first goal. And to help others become what they are capable of becoming is my second goal. The two goals are synergistic — they are mutually reinforcing.

"As I mature in my philosophical thinking, the single trait that I have come to appreciate the most is authenticity. Isn't it wonderful when one has the opportunity to interact with another person who is completely authentic. There are no facades and no hidden agendas. The person is simply himself or herself. Oh, that there could be more authentic persons in the world.

"Building on the notion of authenticity, I am committed to a life of dialogue. I want to engage in honest and open communication with other persons. I want to engage in a mutual search for truth and wisdom with other persons. In the process, I would like to help lift others to their higher selves — and at the same time be lifted to my higher self. This is living life on a very high plane.

"In brief, these views reflect my philosophy of life. I could spend quite some time elaborating on these ideas, but I believe that I have highlighted the central themes. I hope that I have been clear in communicating them.

"You asked me earlier what I would like to have written as my epitaph. Indeed, a thought-provoking question. In the fewest words possible, it would be 'Jody was Jody'."

This, then, describes the person who has reached the fourth rung of the ladder — the level of Existenz. Anyone who has a philosophical orientation to life no doubt can relate very well to the ideas expressed here.

What is the meaning of truth for a person who has worked his or her way up to the level of Existenz? Jaspers replies that "Existenz only becomes apparent and thereby real if it comes to itself through *existential communication* with another Existenz."[59, p.92] When one authentic person is engaged in genuine dialogue with another authentic person in a mutual search for truth, these two persons are experiencing a very genuine form of truth. There is absolutely nothing that can replace this form of truth.

Jaspers states it well when he says:

> Truth therefore cannot be separated from communicability.
> It only appears in time as a reality-through-communication.
> Abstracted from communication, truth hardens into un-
> reality. The movement of communication is at one and the
> same time the preservation of, and the search for, the
> truth.[59, pp.79-80]

In this mutual search for truth, one Existenz is engaged in a dialogue with another Existenz. The bond that unites them is *reason* — the subject to which we turn next.

REASON

The person who has achieved the level of Existenz — or, we can say, "lives out of the Encompassing"— is guided by reason. Manifold are the four modes of being. What connects these modes of being is reason.

The role of reason is elucidated by Jaspers:

> Inextricably bound to Existenz is something else which con-
> cerns the connection of all these modes of being. This is
> no new whole, but rather a continuing demand and move-
> ment. It is the *bond* which unites all modes of being; it is
> called reason. . . . Reason is the *total will to communica-
> tion*. It wants to turn toward everything that is capable of
> expression, toward everything that is, in order to preserve
> it.[59, p.64]

Jaspers stresses that the basic characteristic of reason is the will to unity. Reason moves beyond the unity of consciousness at large (understanding) and the unity of spirit (compelling ideas) to an all-embracing unity. It is reason that clarifies the four modes of the En-compassing, that then prevents their isolation, and presses on toward the union of all the modes of the Encompassing.

Jaspers also makes special note of the connection between reason and Existenz:

> The great poles of our being, which encounter one another
> in every mode of the Encompassing, are thus reason and
> Existenz. They are inseparable. Existenz only becomes clear
> through reason; reason only has content through Existenz.
> Without reason, Existenz is inactive, sleeping, and as though
> not there. Each disappears with the disappearance of the
> other.[59, pp.67-68]

Over the ages, reason has had a difficult road to travel. There have been numerous obstacles. Just to name a few: the reign of totalitarianism rather than democracy, the encouragement of obedience rather than independent thinking, the personal security found in superstition and magic, the unwillingness of people to bare their innermost thoughts, the insistence on being right at all costs, the belief that there is only one path to truth, the lack of openness to differing points of view, and the use of manipulation rather than persuasion. Yet, in spite of these obstacles, reason is still manifest in the lives of many.

Living out of the Encompassing requires the use of reason. Thus, it is important that we consider some of its salient features.

Reason is a striving for unity in one's thinking. Each thinking person is bombarded with multitudinous facts and concepts. Oftentimes these elements of thought are diffuse and contradictory. Reason endeavors to consolidate these disparate facts and concepts into a meaningful whole.

Reason is open to all. It is not the exclusive property of the professional philosopher. Reason is available to each person who wishes to question and to use his or her rational powers in the search for answers.

Reason assumes that there is no monopoly of truth. No individual or group has exclusive possession of truth, which is available to all of us — regardless of our professional, political, or religious leanings.

Reason is constantly on the move. It questions, searches, tests, and answers. And the answers often are considered to be only tentative — to be revised as better answers are uncovered. Reason advances, moves to a plateau, and then advances to a higher plateau. This steadfast movement is the very nature of reason.

Reason subjects itself to criticism. Never arriving at a state of completion, reason is constantly in the process of achieving ever-closer approximations of truth. With this in mind, persons of reason will search out those who will challenge and disagree. And even unjustified criticism may be of value.

And finally, reason is the connecting link between all persons. How do we make real contact with those individuals of different historical origins, who may speak a different language, and who may even be our adversaries? This contact can come about through reason. If two parties are willing to make a genuine commitment to the use of reason in working through their points of disagreement, there is a real possibility of arriving at mutually agreeable solutions. Without reason, all is lost.

In sum, we can heed the words of Karl Jaspers when he pays his respects to reason:

> I can speak of reason, personify it, and pay my respects to it as the condition of all truth for me. But it is never a permanent thing; rather it constitutes a continuous task in time. It is not an end in itself, but rather a medium. It is that through which everything else preserves its nature, is clarified, corroborated, and recognized. It is as though without reason everything were asleep like a seed.[59, p.131]

SUMMING UP

The purpose of this chapter has been to present Jaspers' idea of the Encompassing as a framework for a comprehensive theory of ethics. Why Jaspers? The framework provided by this renowned German philosopher may be the only one that is sufficiently comprehensive to do justice to the various ethical systems — to elucidate them, to integrate them, and to incorporate them in a practical decision making strategy. Importantly, the Encompassing is grounded in human nature and values — which indeed should be the cornerstone of any comprehensive ethical system. Further, the Encompassing reflects human nature and values in the *real world* — not in some "ought" that whirls freely in the sky.

Just to review, the Encompassing includes four modes of being: empirical existence, consciousness at large, spirit, and Existenz. These modes of being are arranged in a hierarchical order: with empirical existence at the bottom rung of the ladder, we move up to consciousness at large, then to spirit, and finally to Existenz. The bond that unites the four modes of being is reason. Each person has his or her own Encompassing.

The Encompassing points up what happens when individuals become completely stuck at one level of being. This means that the individual is fixated at one level without any substantial connections with other levels. At the level of empirical existence we find the pure hedonist who is seeking pleasure and avoiding pain, lacking any moral or religious values. At the level of consciousness at large we find the scientist who has converted science into scientism, treating science as a pseudo-religion. At the level of spirit we find the "true believer," convinced that one particular religion or political view is the only way to truth. And at the level of Existenz we find the "rebel without a cause," guided only by unquestioned impulse and whim. This brief analysis provides a clear message to each and to all: do not become suffocated in a single mode of being.

The notion of the Encompassing provides a framework for the development of a meaningful theory of ethics — and an answer to Socrates' question of how one should live. A major contribution of this framework is the elucidation of the meaning of integrity.

The leader-manager who consistently makes right-good decisions is a person of integrity. Most people agree that they admire leaders who display integrity. But when we probe to uncover their meaning of integrity, we come away with a variety of definitions. Inasmuch as integrity lies at the heart of ethics, it is important that we arrive at an acceptable definition.

We can consider two common definitions of integrity:

1. A driving force in the movement toward *consistency* between values and action, or between espoused theory and theory-in-use. (Steven Kerr, "Integrity in Effective Leadership"[70])

2. As a synthesizing form of thought, integrity acts *to preserve the whole* by accepting polarities, appreciating differences, and finding connections that transcend and encompass all points of view. (Suresh Srivastva and David Cooperrider, "The Urgency for Executive Integrity," in Srivastva and Associates[117].)

These are two very different meanings of integrity. The first is analytical, and the second is synthetic. We need to look at both.

Focusing on the first definition, we can concoct illustrations of *consistency between values and actions* at each level of being:

- **Empirical existence.** "As a merchant who is profit-driven, I will consistently short-change my customers so that I will show a substantial profit at the end of each month — and then move out before the sheriff arrives."
- **Consciousness at large.** "As the head of the Security Department, I will consistently enforce the rules even if, at times, they may be misdirected."
- **Spirit.** "As a loyal employee, I will consistently abide by the norms of my company even though some of my best friends believe that I am working for a shady organization."

- **Existenz.** "As a free thinker, I will consistently abide by the dictates of my conscience regardless of consequences, rules, or social norms."

Indeed, these examples do satisfy the first definition of integrity: consistency between values and actions. But something is terribly amiss. Through the above examples it is clear that this definition is neither intuitively nor logically satisfying. We obviously need a broader and more acceptable definition of integrity.

Let's consider the second definition of integrity: a synthesizing form of thought that acts to *preserve the whole* by accepting polarities, appreciating differences, and finding connections that transcend and encompass all points of view.

This second definition has a very nice ring to it. Of course! This definition captures the essence of the Encompassing. It is an *Encompassing view of integrity.* Eureka! We have found a definition of integrity that fits like a glove.

The distinction between these two meanings of integrity is noted by Roger Harrison:

> At any given time, the expression of one's integrity is in being fully who one is at that time. But the process, what I have called the search for integrity, consists in being willing and able to move on from where one is to the next phase of the process. Thus, one can have integrity and at the same time be completely stuck, unable to comprehend the possibility of a further development beyond the current state.[50, p.60]

What does all this mean? Simply this: if we define integrity in terms of consistency between values and actions, we will end up with an unduly restricted system of ethics. But if we define integrity in terms of the Encompassing—which includes the entire hierarchy of modes of being guided by reason—we will arrive at a comprehensive system of ethics, one that should bear more fruit.

This, then, is the cornerstone postulate of our proposed theory of ethics: *the person of true integrity lives out of the Encompassing.* This is the person who has advanced to the level of Existenz, while still "being at home" in the modes of spirit, consciousness at large, and empirical existence, and is guided by reason. This is the person whose life is represented by a complete ladder: all four rungs are present and are held firmly in place by two sides. This is the person who best represents what is meant by the appellation "a fully functioning human being."

A corollary to this postulate is that there are four clearly identified levels of moral development. Consistent with the modes of being embedded within the Encompassing, we can delineate these levels of moral development:

- Level I (empirical existence): seeking pleasure and avoiding pain, with the locus of authority found in expected consequences.
- Level II (consciousness at large): abiding by rules and laws, with the locus of authority found in the generator and the enforcer of the rules and laws.
- Level III (spirit): conforming to social customs and norms, with the locus of authority found in the general will of the community.
- Level IV (Existenz): living by the dictates of one's conscience, with the locus of authority found in reason.

In the vast literature on ethics are several well-documented and empirically-based theories of moral development. But these tend to focus on stages of moral development in children.* It would seem that what is presented here as four levels of moral development derived from the Encompassing would be more useful in describing and understanding moral development in adults.

In sum, the idea of the Encompassing can provide a framework for the development of a comprehensive theory of ethics. The Encompassing elucidates human nature and values, the meaning of integrity, and levels of moral development. With this knowledge in hand, we can now move to an examination of the various ethical systems and the role of each in a comprehensive theory of ethics.

---

*See, for example, Lawrence Kohlberg's *Essays on Moral Development* (Vol. II) *The Psychology of Moral Development* (New York: Harper and Row, 1985).

IV

Ethical Systems

When a businessman, or any person living in this complex
and highly developed stage of civilization, tries to be ethical,
he has a much more difficult task than is usually assumed.
He has to choose which set of ethics he is going to employ.
He has to make decisions, not merely between the good and
the bad in a popular sense, but between various kinds of
goodness as well, to determine their appropriateness in the
total situation of which he is a part.

Samuel Miller
"The Tangle of Ethics"[89]

---

*The Nature of Ethics • End-Result Ethics • Rule Ethics • Social Contract
Ethics • Personalistic Ethics • Summing Up*

THE NATURE OF ETHICS

"What does 'ethical' mean to you?" This was the question posed to
100 business people by Raymond Baumhart.[8, pp.11-12]. Here are some
of the typical responses:
- "Before coming to the interview, to make sure that I knew what
  we would talk about, I looked up 'ethics' in my dictionary.
  I read it and can't understand it. I don't know what the concept means."
- "'Ethical' is what my feelings tell me is right. But this is not
  a fixed standard, and that makes the problem."
- "'Ethical' means accepted standards in terms of your personal
  and social welfare, what you believe is right."

It is no simple matter to define ethics. The literature on the subject reveals a number of different definitions, and some of the differences are substantial.

In the book, *Above the Bottom Line,* Solomon and Hanson offer a general definition of ethics that is consistent with Socratic thinking:

> *Ethics* is, first of all, the quest for, and the understanding of, the good life, living well, a life worth living. It is largely a matter of perspective: putting every activity and goal in its place, knowing what is worth doing and what is not worth doing, knowing what is worth wanting and having and knowing what is not worth wanting and having.[116. p 9]

An *ethical system* may be defined as "a set of interrelated values concerning preferable modes of conduct." In the language of M. Scott Peck, your personal ethical system is your "map" of the good life. In the language of Mark Pastin,[100] your ethical system is your set of "ground rules" for making what you consider to be a "right" decision.

To pursue the idea of "ground rules for making right decisions," consider the following quotation by the former president of the University of Notre Dame, Father Theodore Hesburgh:

> My basic principle is that you don't make decisions because they are easy, you don't make them because they are cheap, you don't make them because they are popular; you make them because they are right. Not distinguishing between rightness and wrongness is where administrators get into trouble.[53. p.172]

As a point of departure in my Ethics and Leadership seminar, I have asked the participants to reflect on Father Hesburgh's quotation and then answer this question: What ground rules do you follow in determining what is a "right" decision? The responses are quite varied and tend to fall into four distinct categories. These are typical responses that represent the four categories:

- "I would make the decision on the basis of *expected results,* what would give us the greatest return on investment."
- "I would make the decision on the basis of *what the law says,* on the legality of the matter."
- "I would make the decision on the basis of the *strategy* and *values* of my organization."
- "I would make the decision on the basis of my *personal convictions* and what my conscience told me to do."

The four illustrative responses represent four distinctly different ethical systems: end-result ethics, rule ethics, social contract ethics, and personalistic ethics. It will be instructive to examine each of these four ethical systems and then consider the role that each might play in a comprehensive ethical theory.

These particular ethical systems have been selected because, in addition to achieving noteworthy status in the philosophy of ethics, each reflects a different mode of being. While there are other ethical systems not to be considered here, an understanding of these four will provide a reasonably broad perspective of different approaches to ethics.

The four ethical systems to be examined are defined as follows:

Ethical System	Proponent	Definition
End-result ethics	John Stuart Mill (1806–1873)	The moral rightness of an action is determined by considering its consequences.
Rule ethics	Immanuel Kant (1724–1804)	The moral rightness of an action is determined by laws and standards
Social contract ethics	Jean Jacques Rousseau (1712–1778)	The moral rightness of an action is determined by the customs and norms of a particular community.
Personalistic ethics	Martin Buber (1878–1965)	The moral rightness of an action is determined by one's conscience.

Figure 15. Principal ethical systems.

- **End-result ethics:** The moral rightness of an action is determined by considering its consequences. (Principal exponents: Jeremy Bentham and John Stuart Mill.)
- **Rule ethics:** The moral rightness of an action is determined by laws and standards. (Prominent exponent: Immanuel Kant.)
- **Social contract ethics:** The moral rightness of an action is determined by the customs and norms of a particular society or community. (Principal exponent: Jean Jacques Rousseau.)
- **Personalistic ethics:** The moral rightness of an action is determined by one's conscience. (Prominent exponent: Martin Buber.)

What criteria should be used in evaluating a particular ethical system? In his book, *Ethics: Theory and Practice*, Jacques Thiroux provides us with a list of attributes of a workable and livable ethical system:

1. It should be rationally based and yet not devoid of emotion.
2. It should be as logically consistent as possible but not rigid and inflexible.
3. It must have universality or general application to all humanity and yet be applicable in a practical way to particular individuals and situations.
4. It should be able to be taught and promulgated.
5. It must have the ability to resolve conflicts among human beings, duties, and obligations.

As you read the summaries of the four ethical systems on the following pages, consider how well each one satisfies the criteria delineated by Thiroux.[118, p. 145]

END-RESULT ETHICS

Large numbers of people throughout the world subscribe to end-result ethics (which is known to many as "utilitarianism"). The reason for the large following is that this particular ethical system is pragmatic: it is a practical approach to problems and affairs, it focuses on consequences, and it appeals to one's common sense.

Jeremy Bentham (1748–1832) an English philosopher and the founder of the ethical doctrine known as utilitarianism, captures the essence of end-result ethics in these words:

Nature has placed mankind under the governance of two
sovereign masters, *pain* and *pleasure*. It is for them alone
to point out what we ought to do, as well as to determine
what we shall do. On the one hand the standard of right
and wrong, on the other the chain of causes and effects,
are fastened to their throne. They govern us in all we do,
in all we say, in all we think: every effort we can make to
throw off our subjection, will serve but to demonstrate and
confirm it.[14]

This quotation, which is taken from Bentham's *Principles of
Morals and Legislation* (1789), is the cornerstone of end-result ethics.
It is seen that the focus is on seeking pleasure and avoiding pain —
the two touchstones of end-result ethics.

Whenever we face difficult choices, according to Bentham, we
can translate a dilemma into a problem of addition and subtraction.
Consider a man or woman contemplating marriage. A table such
as that shown in Figure 16 might be drawn up. A pure utilitarian
would then choose the alternative that offered the greatest total of
pleasure. (Would you ever make an important decision this way?)

Bentham's basic philosophy of utilitarianism — or end-result
ethics — was embellished and promoted by his godson, John Stuart
Mill (1806–1873). The ten principles of end-result ethics that follow
are taken from Mill's *Utilitarianism*.[88]

IF I MARRY	UNITS OF PLEASURE	IF I DON'T MARRY	UNITS OF PLEASURE
1. Secure sex life	+1000	1. Freedom to enter new	
2. But no playing the field	− 300	relationships	+ 500
3. The joy of children	+ 700	2. Loneliness	− 300
4. The expense of children	− 300	3. No children, no grand-	
5. Companionship in old age	+ 400	children	− 800
6. Responsibilities, ties,		4. But no responsibilities	+1000
burdens	− 600	5. No ties to hold me in one	
		job, one place	+ 400
		6. But no roots, no one who	
		really cares whether I	
		live or die	− 500
THE UTILITY OF MARRYING	+ 700	THE UTILITY OF NOT MARRYING	+ 300
+700 IS GREATER THAN +300, THEREFORE: I DO			

Robert Paul Wolff, *About Philosophy*, p. 69.
Reprinted with permission (129).

Figure 16. To marry or not to marry — a utilitarian calculation.

1. **To determine if an action is right or wrong, one must concentrate on its likely consequences.***

   Is this particular action right or wrong? How am I to judge? I cannot appeal to laws and standards. I cannot appeal to the customs and norms of the community. Nor can I appeal to my conscience. I can appeal only to the probable consequences. What are the likely effects or outcomes of my action? This alone will provide me the answer.

2. **Rules of action must take their character from the end to which they are subservient.**

   End-result ethics will incorporate rules into its ethical doctrine, but the *source* of the rules is different from that of other ethical systems. In the case of end-result ethics, the source is found in the expected results. Consider, for example, the rationale for reducing the speed limit on the highways from 70 m.p.h. to 55 m.p.h. Why? The answer is simple and straightforward: the reduced speed limit is expected to save a given number of lives each year. The rule is based upon the end which it serves.

3. **Actions are right in proportion as they tend to promote happiness, wrong as they tend to produce the reverse of happiness.**

   Now we have a stationary target that will help us judge our actions as being either right or wrong. Perhaps it is not always stationary, but at least it is a target. And we are freed from a binary or dichotomous mind-set (i.e., "right" vs. "wrong") by being able to judge our actions *in proportion* as they tend to promote happiness—thus allowing us to place actions on a continuum from "very undesirable" to "very desirable."

4. **Happiness may be defined as the presence of pleasure and the absence of pain.**

   The notion of happiness may seem amorphous, but the utilitarians provide us with a definition. Individuals are happy to the extent that they experience pleasure and are unhappy to the extent that they experience pain. It would then follow that

---

*Throughout the chapter, the principle in boldface type is almost verbatim from the designated author, but the elaboration of the principle is my own.

the happiest of all people would be that individual who experiences only pleasure and no pain.

5. **Since each person desires his or her own happiness, this is sufficient reason to posit happiness as an ultimate end.**

It would be difficult to argue with the premise that each person desires his or her own happiness — that is, to seek pleasure and to avoid pain. This is simply basic human nature. Inasmuch as *every person* seeks happiness, it would then follow that happiness is the *ultimate* end for all living persons. And "ultimate" means the acme, the summit, the very highest. There is nothing any higher on the scale of ends.

6. **Because happiness is the sole end of human action, the promotion of it is the criterion of morality.**

In order to judge an action as being moral or ethical, we obviously need a criterion — or standard — on which to base our judgment. Given that happiness is the ultimate end of human actions, it then follows that the promotion of happiness is the obvious standard for judging actions as being either moral or immoral, or even better, the *degree to which* the actions are moral or immoral.

7. **The happiness that determines what is right in conduct is not the agent's own happiness, but that of all concerned.**

This principle calls upon the agent to make decisions as an "independent observer" in judging the likely effects of a particular action on *all stakeholders* — that is, on all parties that might be affected by the action. It is this principle that prevents utilitarianism from being essentially hedonistic or egoistic. The focus on "the happiness of all concerned" manifests a humanistic orientation.

8. **An action has utility to the extent that it can produce happiness or prevent unhappiness.**

Bentham defines utility as "that property in any object, whereby it tends to produce benefit, advantage, pleasure, good, or happiness, or to prevent the happening of mischief, pain, evil, or unhappiness to the party whose interest is considered."[14, p.34]

This definition should be expanded to include "that property in any object *or action* . . ."

9. **An action is right from an ethical point of view if and only if the sum total of utilities produced by that act is greater than the sum total of utilities produced by any other act the agent could have performed in its place.**

This principle gives us a quantitative framework for making ethical decisions. Consider an individual who is faced with an ethical dilemma involving a choice between two undesirable alternatives. The instruction here is to simply identify the utilities associated with each alternative (giving due consideration to all affected parties), add the utilities for each alternative, and then select the alternative that yields the largest sum total of utilities. This type of logic apparently was used in arriving at the decision to increase the maximum speed limit on U.S. highways from 55 m.p.h. to 65 m.p.h.

10. **Utility serves as the common umpire in choosing between incompatible moral obligations.**

Any objective-minded person would like to remove subjectivity and bias from ethical decisions. Also, such a person no doubt would like to assure fairness to all affected parties. The concept of utility provides the answer. This is the "common umpire" that promises both objectivity and fairness. Thus, it is no longer an issue of "my views versus your views." Rather, it is simply a matter of calculating the utilities and then making a decision accordingly.

These ten principles constitute the core of the ethical doctrine known as utilitarianism — or what we are calling end-result ethics. The principles form a coherent whole — they are clear, logical, and all of a piece. There are many devoted, enthusiastic supporters of this ethical system. But one can also find large numbers of antagonists who have serious reservations about the value and usefulness (or "utility") of end-result ethics. Some of the thought-provoking questions most often raised by the skeptics are presented below.

How does one define happiness, pleasure, and utility? The utilitarians tend to use such terms as happiness, pleasure, and utility as though these were universally meaningful concepts. But our own experience tells us that what constitutes happiness and pleasure for one person might be just the opposite for another. Consider, for example, a woman who nightly scrubs office floors. Could she be happy during this eight-hour night shift? Does she derive any pleasure from this drudgery? Many would respond, "No." But suppose we find that this noble lady is working at this job to put her handicapped child through college. Then we note that within her own self-being there may be happiness and pleasure — even during this backbreaking work. Yet it is incomprehensible to the observer.

How does one go about measuring happiness, pleasure, and utility? During the time of the heavy debates concerning the proposed speed limit increase from 55 m.p.h. to 65 m.p.h., I recall reading an article that presented a purely utilitarian argument. The author, who had marshalled a large amount of data to support his position that the speed limit should be increased, compared the total amount of time that would be saved by millions of American drivers to the total amount of time that would be "lost" by the unfortunate ones who might be killed. As might be expected, the data overwhelmingly supported the faster speed limit. But the argument was based upon at least two tenuous assumptions: first, that it is reasonable to compare wasted time in driving to wasted time in not living, and second, that the time spent in driving is wasted. (Many drivers would confirm that they use this time productively: reflecting, planning, unwinding, listening to music or instructional tapes, etc.) Because of these questionable assumptions, how do we measure utility in this particular case — or in most cases involving ethical issues?

How does one predict the outcome of a particular action? In end-result ethics, to determine if an action is right or wrong, one must concentrate on its likely consequences. Easy to say, but often difficult to do. Say we are faced with two alternatives in an ethical dilemma and we are called upon to predict the likely consequences associated with each alternative. But suppose that this is the first time that we have ever been faced with this particular dilemma and that we have no data or previous experience on which to base our prediction. What then?

How does one choose between short-term happiness and long-term happiness? Another principle of end-result ethics tells us that actions are right in proportion as they tend to promote happiness, wrong as they tend to produce the reverse of happiness. But what about time frame? Most adults — at least psychologically mature adults — have been faced time and again with situations in which they felt compelled to sacrifice short-term pleasure for long-term happiness. But if they do this repeatedly and over an extended period of time, they may suffer from a happiness-is-out-there-in-the-future syndrome: they are unable to stop and smell the roses today. Thus, it is reasonable to ask: What is the time frame for happiness? Might it even extend beyond the agent's own lifetime in the sense that a given action, which causes distress and discomfort to the agent, nevertheless is expected to benefit the agent's children or perhaps the children's children? A tough call.

If 90 percent of the people were free and 10 percent were slaves, would this satisfy the Greatest Happiness Principle? This is one of the favorite questions raised by the anti-utilitarians. Assuming that the 90 percent who are free can benefit from the services of the slaves, then we can chalk up a certain number of positive utilities. And the 10 percent who must remain in slavery will yield a certain number of negative utilities. But because of the large differential in numbers, the positive utilities outweigh the negative utilities. Hence, the conclusion is that the state of slavery for only 10 percent of the population is justified. According to the Greatest Happiness Principle, the logic appears irrefutable. But it leaves us with the uneasy feeling that something is amiss (regardless of whether or not we would happen to be in the 10 percent).

If you could sit in a pleasure-inducing booth the remainder of your life, would you choose to do so? Just imagine this electronically-controlled booth! You are seated in a comfortable reclining chair that also serves as your bed. The electrodes are attached to your head, and the panel of controls is at your disposal. You name it — whatever you want — just punch the appropriate button on the control panel. Immediately you will receive the desired sensory pleasure in whatever intensity and for whatever duration requested. And you can spend the remainder of your days in the booth. ... I have presented this question to a number of persons and have yet to find one who is interested in taking advantage of the opportunity. I get such responses as "It would become boring after a while." ... "There would be no challenge in life." Alas, does this mean that the seeking of pleasure, after all, is not the ultimate goal?

We could continue with additional examples that challenge the validity of end-result ethics, but these few should serve to confirm our position that end-result ethics has both strengths and limitations.

End-result ethics does indeed have distinctive strengths. For example: it is practical; it focuses on consequences; it takes into consideration the various stakeholders; it offers a certain amount of rigor to the rather nebulous field of ethics; and it appeals to one's common sense. These advantages cannot be dismissed lightly.

But it is clear that end-result ethics also has distinct limitations. For example: it proposes that we seek greater pleasure and happiness but gives us little direction; it is unable to provide universally acceptable definitions of pleasure and happiness; and it promises a certain rigor — such as measuring pleasure in terms of utility — that is relevant to the economic dimension of decision making but comes up short when applied to the ethical dimension. These limitations bring the doctrine into question.

What can we conclude from this analysis? It is simply this: end-result ethics is found lacking as a complete theory of ethics but can make a significant contribution to the whole. In other words, it does not constitute a total map of the good life but is an important segment of the total map.

RULE ETHICS

People are faced with rules throughout their lives. The child hears from the parent: "Be sure to say 'thank you'." ... "Always flush." The student hears from the teacher: "You must raise your hand to get permission to leave the classroom." ... "Do your own work." The employee hears from the employer: "Expense reports are to be an accurate reflection of actual expenses." ... "All frequent flier awards are to be turned into the company." The elderly person upon entering the retirement center hears from the center management: "You must be completely honest in reporting your net worth." ... "All visitors must leave by 10:00 p.m."

And so it goes. It sometimes seems that one's entire life is governed by rules. Though we may sometimes complain, we realize that rules are essential to the survival of any community — be it an organization, a village, or a society.

Rule ethics is the second of the four principal ethical doctrines to be examined. It differs substantially from end-result ethics and deserves serious consideration.

A prominent proponent of rule ethics has been Immanuel Kant (1724–1804), the renowned philosopher from Königsberg (in northern

Prussia). Many are those who would agree that the two greatest philosophers of all time are Plato and Kant, with Plato the representative of ancient times and Kant of modern times. Both were committed to a life of reason.

Kant stressed that moral principles must be established on purely rational grounds, falling in the same domain as scientific principles — they lend themselves to criticism and defense. He believed that the truths of ethics had been known for thousands of years and that these truths were objective and universally valid. It then follows that the real moral problem for each person is to struggle to abide by these truths in the face of all the temptations and daemonic forces.

This quotation from Kant captures the essence of rule ethics:

> Rules of ethics are measuring-rules of action and ought to set before us the standard of moral necessity. They ought not to be trimmed in consideration of man's capacity. Any system of ethics which accommodates itself to what man can do corrupts the moral perfection of humanity. The moral law must be pure.[65, p.74]

The rules of ethics are the lodestone — the magnet that attracts. These rules serve as the standard by which each person may judge his or her own actions. To the extent that a person abides by the rules of ethics, it can be said that this person has lived a good life.

The ten principles that follow are intended to serve as a capsule summary of Kant's rule ethics. These principles have been taken primarily from two of Kant's works: *Groundwork of the Metaphysic of Morals*[64] and *Lectures on Ethics.*[65]

1. **All moral concepts have their seat and origin in reason completely *a priori*, and therefore cannot be abstracted from any empirical knowledge.**

    Ethics can be described in terms of the relation between the "is" and the "ought." The "is" constitutes the empirical: what people *actually do*. The "ought" constitutes the rational: presumptive ideas of what people *should do*. The "ought" cannot be derived from the "is." (For example, the fact that 80 percent of the population behave in a certain way does not make it right.) But rather, the "is" should be derived from the "ought." (Which means that human conduct should be guided by moral principles.)

2. **We may act from grounds of compulsion (jurisprudence) or from those of the intrinsic goodness of the action (ethics).**

According to this principle, the civil law represents the bare minimum of ethics. The truly ethical is at a much higher level than the merely legal. A particular individual, for instance, might stay within the law but nevertheless be considered unethical. On the other hand, a second individual might question and challenge specific laws — because they are inhumane laws — but nevertheless be considered an ethical person. The second person is guided by "higher laws"— that is, moral principles that transcend civil laws.

3. **Individuals should take their stand on principles and restrain themselves by rules.**

A set of basic principles and rules should serve as the moral compass for each individual. Fundamental moral principles have been known to humankind for thousands of years. It is the duty of each person to learn these moral principles and to then live in accordance with them. Every person needs direction and guidance for judging right and wrong, and the only way that this direction and guidance can be provided is through moral principles and rules.

4. **To practice virtue is to act on principles.**

Virtue is defined as "moral excellence, righteousness, uprightness, rectitude." This, according to Kant, defines the good life. The only way to live the good life — to practice virtue — is to act on principles. The individual who is an opportunist is not virtuous. The individual who is a manipulator is not virtuous. The individual who is governed only by the external situation is not virtuous. To be considered a virtuous person, one must live from the inside-out: an internal core of moral principles guides the person's actions.

5. **The ultimate good is a life of virtue rather than a life of pleasure.**

Here is where we see a sharp difference between end-result ethics and rule ethics. While end-result ethics presumes that the highest good is a life of pleasure, rule ethics presumes that the highest good is a life of virtue. According to rule ethics, a life of virtue should be one's ultimate goal: all other goals are subordinate to and should contribute to this goal. In the language of Paul Tillich, a life of virtue should be one's "ultimate concern."

6. **Virtue is an Idea, and we should all strive to attain as near as possible to the Idea.**

Virtue is an Idea of what constitutes the good life, an Idea of moral excellence. In its pure sense, we can consider the Idea of moral excellence to be a "10" (on a 10-point scale). Now no mortal can ever achieve a "10"— at least over an extended period of time — but nevertheless can continually strive to move up the scale in the direction of the "10." Over the long haul, there inevitably will be lapses and regressions, but these should spur one to recover, correct, and advance toward the Idea of moral excellence.

7. **Individuals should evaluate themselves by comparing themselves with the Idea of perfection, not by comparing themselves with others.**

In the words of Kant: "The Idea of perfection is a proper standard, and if we measure our worth by it, we find that we fall short of it and feel that we must exert ourselves to come nearer to it; but if we compare ourselves with others, much depends upon who those others are and how they are constituted, and we can easily believe ourselves to be of great worth if those with whom we set up comparisons are rogues."[65, p.215]

8. **We should beware of adjusting the moral law to fit our own actions; rather, we should adjust our actions to fit the moral law.**

The ethics equation includes a constant and a variable. The constant is the Idea of moral perfection, and the variable is our own conduct. We must avoid the trap of rationalizing our actions by adjusting the moral law to fit the actions. On the contrary, we must adjust our actions to fit the moral law. Indeed, we must be ever mindful of which is the constant and which is the variable.

9. **Act as if the principles underlying your action were to become a general law for all of humankind.**

Kant's famous categorical imperative is an example of a rule that can serve as a standard for moral conduct. This rule — or metarule — is indeed profound. Kant viewed it as a more precise philosophical statement of the Golden Rule: "Do unto others as you would have them do unto you." And he considered the rule to be universally valid: it applies to all people in all lands and at all times. In everyday language, this is what the rule says: behave in such a way that whatever you do might become a general law — or standard — for all people. What a heavy responsibility this rule imposes on each individual person! But consider what kind of world we might have if every person would live in accordance with this rule.

10. **Always treat others as ends in themselves, never merely as a means.**

This is Kant's famous practical imperative that can serve as a second example of a rule for moral conduct. It presumes that each individual is a unique human being having worth and dignity. Certainly, there are times when we use others as means to meet our own personal ends — say, store clerks, cab drivers, carpenters, barbers and hairdressers, etc. But we should not treat them *merely* as a means. In all cases, they should be treated with dignity and respect — as unique human beings who are ends in themselves. Wouldn't it be a beautiful world if everyone would live in accordance with this rule?

These ten principles convey Kant's key notions about ethics. They do not represent the entire breadth and depth of this renowned philosopher's thinking on the subject, but they provide a summary of the ideas and spirit of rule ethics.

Not everyone will agree with these ten principles. Some people would have serious reservations about the entire set of principles as well as the underlying premises. Following are some of the common questions raised by the critics of rule ethics.

By what authority do we accept particular rules and the goodness of these rules? I like Kant's rule — or categorical imperative — that I should "act as if the principles underlying my actions were to become a general law for all of humankind." But by what authority do I accept it? Do I accept it simply because Kant said it? No, because there are other affirmations of Kant's that I do not accept. If I accept it on the basis of expected consequences, then I tilt toward end-result ethics. If I accept it on the basis of the customs and norms of my community, then I show a preference for social contract ethics. And if I accept it strictly on the basis of my conscience, then I give top priority to personalistic ethics. But if I am to remain within the domain of rule ethics, I am at a loss to know the locus of authority for the acceptance of a particular rule.

What rule do we follow in choosing between conflicting rules? Assume that you believe in two particular rules of conduct. One pertains to always being considerate of others' feelings, and the second pertains to always telling the truth. Now a friend asks you a straightforward question that calls for a straightforward answer. If you tell the truth, you will hurt your friend's feelings. And if you tell a lie, you have violated one of your guiding principles. Thus, you are forced to choose between two conflicting rules. Which one would you choose? And what rule would you use to guide your choice?

How do we adapt general rules to fit specific situations? Certainly, we must give credence to the rule of being considerate of others' feelings. But suppose we find ourselves in a situation in which we are forced to deal with an out-and-out scoundrel. Do we modify the rule in this case? Certainly, we must give credence to the rule of being honest. But suppose we again find ourselves in a situation in which complete honesty would cause undue stress to our friend. Do we also modify the rule in this case? And now we are faced with an important underlying question: If we find ourselves constantly bending the rules to fit specific situations, might we eventually lose sight of the original set of rules?

How do rules get changed to deal with changing circumstances? Most people would agree that we are in a rapidly and constantly changing environment. So rules that were once generally accepted are now called into question — they no longer apply. Only the most rigid of people would assume that exactly the same rules that cover all aspects of human conduct should prevail throughout eternity. But how do rules get changed to deal with changing circumstances? In other words, what rule or metarule do we use to change rules?

Why should we follow a given rule if the consequences are likely to be bad? The critics of rule ethics like to pose the following hypothetical situation. Assume that you are a highly ethical person who is committed to always telling the truth. You are now under a great deal of stress because one of your relatives has escaped from a band of evil people and is hiding in your attic. Several of the evil people arrive at your front door and ask you if you know the whereabouts of your relative. Would you tell these evil persons the truth? Probably not. But it is interesting to note that two of the greatest philosophers of all time — Kant and St. Augustine — apparently would feel compelled to tell the truth.

Is there such a thing as a rule with absolutely no exceptions? I frequently pose this question to the participants in my Ethics and Leadership seminar. The ensuing discussion is usually quite lively. First, one participant will present an example of a rule for which there absolutely would be no exceptions — at least for the person presenting the rule. But then other participants will offer specific circumstances that will be sufficiently compelling to convince the first person that there are indeed exceptions to every rule of conduct.

If Kant were alive today, I wonder how he might respond to these basic questions that have been raised by scholars over the past 200 years. It would be difficult to foretell the specifics of his responses, but we could be certain that his responses would be thoughtful — and rational.

This brief analysis has attempted to point up both the strengths and limitations of Kantian rule ethics. And indeed it does have both strengths and limitations.

The major strength of rule ethics is that it offers a structured framework for ethical conduct. It provides basic rules that determine the rightness or wrongness of specific actions. According to Kant, these rules have been in existence for thousands of years and are universally valid. It is the duty of each person to learn the rules and then apply them in his or her daily life. Individuals are thus able to judge their own conduct on the basis of the standards established by the rules. Because of the structure provided, rule ethics is very appealing to those people who dislike ambiguity. Rules provide certainty.

But these strengths are only on the surface. As we probe into the foundation of rule ethics, we find inherent weaknesses. To review, the weaknesses are highlighted in the inability of rule ethics to answer such basic questions as these: (1) By what authority do we accept particular rules and the goodness of these rules? (2) What rule do we follow in choosing between conflicting rules? (3) How do we adapt general rules to fit specific situations? (4) How do rules get changed to deal with changing circumstances? (5) Why should we follow a given rule if the consequences are likely to be bad? (6) Is there such a thing as a rule with absolutely no exceptions? The inability of the

rule ethicists to provide satisfactory answers to these questions brings
the foundation into question.

In sum, it is clear that rule ethics has both strengths and limitations. Because of its nontrivial limitations, rule ethics by itself cannot serve as a complete theory of ethics. Nevertheless, it can make
a significant contribution to the whole. Rule ethics is not the total
map of the good life but is an important segment of the map.

SOCIAL CONTRACT ETHICS

We will begin our examination of social contract ethics with an illustration. Suppose that a group of people banded together to form
an association. The association — as a formal body — is intended to
meet specific needs of the members that cannot be met by the
members acting individually. The members have their initial meeting
to establish the association's bylaws. All members enter into the discussion and agree on a formal set of bylaws. The members then reach
agreement on an important condition: every individual member must
abide by the bylaws, and any significant violation will result in
dismissal from the association. Thus, what is established between the
association and the individual members is a social contract.

Now let's consider a second example — a slightly modified version of the first. The setting is an industrial research laboratory in
which a Ph.D. research scientist has just begun employment. On the
first day of work, the scientist is provided a general orientation by
the immediate supervisor. The purpose of this session is for the supervisor to explain what the company will provide the scientist and what
the scientist is expected to contribute to the company — in other words,
the ground rules. The company will provide resources and opportunities — a competitive salary, modern facilities and equipment,
several technicians to assist the research scientist, and freedom to
publish in the professional journals. And this is what is expected of
the scientist — creative and productive research, documentation of
all research findings, and the signing over of all patent rights to the
company. The scientist agrees with the conditions, shakes hands with
the supervisor, and heads for the laboratory. The supervisor and
research scientist have just established a social contract. (Granted,
the scientist was not a member of the original body that formulated
the company's policies, but inasmuch as the scientist was free to choose

whether or not to work for this particular company, we believe that this example satisfies the general conditions necessary for the establishment of a social contract.)

The father of social contract ethics is Jean Jacques Rousseau (1712–1778). This well known political philosopher was born in Geneva and spent much of his life in Paris.

As a philosopher of the Enlightenment who questioned and challenged absolute kingly authority, Rousseau was constantly in trouble with government authorities. Consequently, he was forced to move from country to country to escape persecution. Even though Rousseau was a highly controversial figure, it is generally agreed that he was one of the great political philosophers.

Rousseau sought an answer to this question: Is there any way in which individual persons can submit to the commands of a legitimate state *without giving up their freedom and autonomy?* After giving much thought to the question, he concluded that the authority of the state could be founded only upon *an agreement among all the individuals who were to be ruled by the state.* To Rousseau, this was the key to balancing freedom and authority. (Essentially, this was the basic rationale underlying the establishment of the U. S. Constitution.)

Rousseau elucidates the essence of social contract ethics in this passage:

> Each of us places in common his person and all his power under the supreme direction of the general will; and as one body we all receive each member as an indivisible part of the whole. ... Man loses by the social contract his natural liberty, and an unlimited right to all which tempts him, and which he can obtain; in return he acquires civil liberty, and proprietorship of all he possesses.[106, p.15, p.19]

This passage includes several key points: (1) each member of the community must act under the authority of the general will; (2) each member is an essential part of the whole; (3) each member gives up a certain amount of freedom by being a part of the collective body; but (4) each member gains a greater amount of freedom through the support and protection of the community.

The basic idea of a social contract is what the legal profession calls *quid pro quo* —"this for that." The individual contributes to the community, and the community contributes to the individual. Each side must stand to benefit from the arrangement to make the contract binding.

The ten principles that follow are intended to serve as a capsule summary of social contract ethics. They are taken from Rousseau's classic work, *The Social Contract*.[106]

1. **People living in a primitive state of nature would perish; therefore, they must be guided by conventions of the general community.**

    Suppose that you have agreed to participate in a survival training program. (You made a wager with a friend during one of your weaker moments.) The big day has now arrived. You will be landed by helicopter on a mountain approximately 100 miles from the nearest community. You will be provided with these supplies: a three-day supply of food and water, a sleeping bag, a raincoat, a knife, and a box of matches. How long do you believe you could survive? Three days? Certainly. Seven days? Maybe. Thirty days? Probably not—unless you are a Daniel Boone or a Jeremiah Johnson. Most of us realize that we could not survive under such conditions for an entire month. And that is why we also realize that we are completely dependent upon the general community for our survival.

2. **The passing from the state of nature to the civil state substitutes justice for instinct and gives to actions a moral character that they lacked before.**

    The individual living in the state of nature—that is, alone in the wilderness—cannot be judged as either moral or immoral. The only appropriate descriptor is *amoral*, because morality is simply not a factor for an individual living alone in the wilderness. *Morality has to do with one's dealings with other human beings.* When this individual leaves the wilderness to become a part of a community of persons, then morality does become a factor in his or her life. To be a part of the community, the individual is expected to be guided not by instinct, but by morality.

3. **The act of association in the general community produces a collective and moral body.**

    Let's now assume that we have a number of individuals who have decided to leave the wilderness and form a community.

These one-time loners have agreed to become a collective body. By becoming a collective body they also have become a *moral body* — a body that is governed by a set of ground rules for judging right and wrong conduct. Without the ground rules there could be no collective body. (The individuals might as well return to the wilderness.) Thus, the set of ground rules constitutes the *social contract* between the individual members and the collective body. And importantly, the set of ground rules constitutes a standard of morality that transcends any standard professed by an individual member acting alone. It has a reality and truth of its own.

4. **Duty and interest equally oblige the general community and the individual members to lend aid to each other.**

   The members of the newly formed community are now guided by a social contract. To fully realize the spirit and conditions of this contract, both the general community and the individual members have important roles to play. The general community is established to enhance the well-being of the individual members. And each individual member has a duty and obligation to contribute to the maintenance and well-being of the general community. The individual members need the general community, and the general community needs the individual members. Neither could exist without the other.

5. **The general will should serve as the ultimate standard for determining what we should do.**

   The general will alone can direct the diverse interests of the community agreeably to the common good. What all these different interests have in common is what forms the common bond. Thus, there must be some point where the people and all their diverse interests unanimously center, or no community can exist. It is on the basis of this common interest alone that the community can be governed.

6. **The social contract gives the general community — or body politic — absolute command over the members of which it is formed.**

   The body politic that represents the general community is responsible for promoting the common good of all members of the community. To this end, the body politic must have authority commensurate with the responsibility — which means that it must have the power to enforce the general will on the individual members of the community. This authority is absolute! It cannot be questioned or challenged by individual members nor can it be superseded by any higher authority. There is no higher court of appeal.

7. **The manners and morals of the general community should serve as the keystone to the arch, while the particular laws serve only as the arch of the curve.**

We must appreciate that the laws of the community are simply a vehicle for codifying the manners and morals of the general community. The manners and morals are the flywheel, and the laws are merely a reflection. For example, if the community as a collective body is opposed to such actions as theft, drunkenness, and adultery, then laws will be passed to prohibit such actions. It is then the duty of every member of the community to abide by and uphold these laws.

8. **The people submit themselves to the laws and ought to enjoy the right of making them.**

We can expect that the manners and morals of a given community will change over time. It is then necessary to adjust the laws so that they are an accurate reflection of the changes in the manners and morals. How do the laws get changed? There is only one way: by the general will of the people through the body politic.

9. **The individual members of the community must consent to all the laws, and even those that are passed in spite of their opposition.**

What kind of community would it be if each member could decide which of the laws he or she wanted to follow? It would indeed be in a chaotic state. Each member is free to speak his or her mind to the appropriate members of the body politic. But once this body establishes a particular law, the law is absolutely binding on every member — even if the member is opposed to it.

10. **Should there be any individuals who oppose the social contract, their opposition will not invalidate it, but only hinder their being included.**

The social contract, being an agreement between the general community and the individual members, establishes a set of ground rules for all members of the community. These ground rules are absolutely binding on all members of the community. Should a minority of individuals oppose the ground rules (and, in turn, the general will), this in no way brings into questions the validity of the ground rules. The problem is not with the ground rules but with the minority of individuals who oppose them. And these individuals have two alternatives: they can either decide to abide by the ground rules or leave the community. There is no other alternative.

In view of these basic principles of social contract ethics, we must agree that Rousseau did indeed work out a logical and coherent ethical system. The principles are internally consistent and, to any democratic-minded person, compelling. Inasmuch as Rousseau's political philosophy had such a great influence on our founding fathers in their establishment of the U. S. Constitution, dare we criticize it? But criticize it we must, because the foundation on which this ethical system is based has a few cracks in it.

The critics have posed a number of thoughtful and penetrating questions that raise doubts about the validity of Rousseau's ethical doctrine. It is worthwhile to consider several of these questions.

How do we determine the general will? According to Rousseau's social contract ethics, the standards of morality for a particular community are to be determined by the general will of the members of that community. This presumption may sound all right in theory, but it is very difficult to put into practice. Consider these current social issues: abortion, gun control, capital punishment, legalization of drugs, euthanasia, just to name a few. The reason why these issues become issues is that the members of the community disagree on their resolution. And disagree they do! So how do we determine the general will? If, for example, we put the issue of gun control up for vote, we may find 45 percent in favor, 40 percent opposed, and 15 percent undecided. The democratic approach would be to go with the 45 percent. But would that represent the general will? Not really.

What is meant by the "common good"? Rousseau tells us, "The first and most important consequence of the principle (social contract ethics) is that the general will alone can direct the forces of the State agreeably to the end of its institution, which is the common good."[106, p.23] This sounds reasonable in theory, but it is difficult to put into practice. The problem lies in determining what constitutes the common good. Consider, for example, the issue of abortion, which continues to be debated in all quarters. Suppose 45 percent of the citizenry are in favor of abortion, 40 percent are opposed, and 15 percent are undecided. Now what is the body politic to do with respect to the establishment of a law that reflects the views of the general community? And whatever the decision, can we conclude that it represents the common good? Very questionable.

What is to be done about the independent thinkers of outspoken opinion? The hallmark of social contract ethics is such notions as the general will, the common good, the social order, the aggregation of forces, the collective body, and above all, unity. To democratic-minded persons, all of these notions have a nice ring to them. But what are their implications for the truly independent thinker, the person of outspoken opinion? Would such a person be viewed as an annoyance, as a thorn in the side of the collective body? Consider the outstanding contributions made by such independent thinkers as Thomas Jefferson, Mahatma Gandhi, and Martin Luther King, Jr. These were leaders of the highest order who challenged the existing social order, who pricked the conscience of the collective body. Might a community that abided strictly by Rousseau's social contract ethics simply ignore or even suppress such independent thinkers? If so, the loser would be the collective body.

According to social contract ethics, would Hitler's Nazi Germany be considered a moral society? Rousseau stresses that the state has sovereignty: "When the State is instituted, residence constitutes consent: to inhabit a territory is to submit to the sovereignty."[106, p. 95] The corollary to this presumption is that there is no law higher than the law of the State. Would it then follow that Hitler's Nazi Germany was a moral state? For purposes of illustration, let's assume that the Nazis were successful in deporting or annihilating all of the Jews and that the remaining Germans were committed to the Nazi Party and the thousand-year Reich. Would this State then satisfy Rousseau's definition of a collective and moral body? If so, such a conclusion is very disconcerting. Something is terribly amiss. And rightly so, as witnessed in the trials of the war criminals in Germany immediately after the end of World War II. Underlying these trials was the belief that there is a code of morality that transcends that which was implicit in Hitler's Nazi Germany. (And now we must ask: What was the ground or authority of this "higher" morality? Or asked in another way: What system of ethics was used to justify the prosecution of the Nazi leaders?)

Is the general community the "measure of all things"? The Sophists in the time of Plato contended that man is the "measure of all things." To the Sophists, standards of morality can be found within man himself, and that it is not necessary or even reasonable to go beyond man himself. It would appear that Rousseau's social contract ethics is an analogous philosophy, but rather than placing the locus of morality in man, it places it in the general community. This means that there is no authority beyond the State that can determine standards of morality for any particular State. Whatever a particular State establishes as morally right is absolute. There is no higher court of appeal.

These are tough questions. And if we wish to include social contract ethics in our comprehensive theory of ethics, they cannot be ignored.

The purpose of this brief analysis has been to highlight both the strengths and limitations of social contract ethics. The obvious strength of this ethical doctrine is that it provides a philosophical base for the establishment of a democratic State — as witnessed in the U. S. Constitution. But we can not allow this strength to eclipse the limitations. And there are at least two: by placing the ultimate authority for morality within the State, social contract ethics leads to ethical relativism; and second, it does not give due consideration to the important role of the independent thinker, the person of outspoken opinion.

Because of these inherent limitations, we must conclude that social contract ethics is not up to the task of serving as a complete theory of ethics. But even though it is not the total map, it is an important segment.

PERSONALISTIC ETHICS

Let's begin our examination of personalistic ethics with an illustration. The setting is an outdoor hotel swimming pool on a warm July morning. At this particular time of day, there are only two persons present — a father, who is fully clothed, sitting in a lounge chair beside the pool and reading a newspaper, and his five-year-old daughter, who is wading in the pool. While the father is engrossed in reading the sports page, he hears his daughter scream for help. She has waded into the deep end of the pool and is struggling to keep her head above water.

At this moment, what is the *right* thing for the father to do? And what system of ethics will he use? If he chooses end-result ethics, he will compare the utilities associated with ruining his clothes, watch, and billfold with those associated with saving his daughter's life. If he chooses rule ethics, he might first check to see if the hotel has posted any rules that prohibit a fully clothed person from entering the pool. And if he chooses social contract ethics, he might reflect on the social compact that he has with his family members. Obviously, he will choose none of these. He will jump into the pool immediately to rescue his daughter.

What we have here is a clear example of personalistic ethics. Without reflecting on consequences, rules, or social compacts, the father simply responds. There is a voice from within that cries, "Act now!"

The voice from within is called "conscience." We hear a person defend a certain action by replying, "I acted according to my conscience." To the daughter leaving for college, we hear the mother urge, "Let your conscience be your guide." We read in the Bible, "His conscience smites him." This heavy-laden word is simply the voice from within that tells one what is right and what is wrong.

The notion of conscience is elucidated by Martin Buber:

> We find the ethical in its purity only there where the human person confronts himself with his own potentiality and decides in this confrontation without asking anything other than what is right and what is wrong in this his own situation.[21, p.95]

Consider carefully what Buber is saying. He captures the essence of personalistic ethics.

Any one of a number of philosophers could have been selected as a proponent of personalistic ethics. I have selected Martin Buber (1878–1965) because he exemplifies personalistic ethics so beautifully in both his writings and his lived life. Most people know of Buber through his philosophy of dialogue, the I-Thou relation. His writings contain rich insight into the nature of the good life and ethics. If

Buber were alive today, he undoubtedly would agree that what we are discussing here is not an ethical "system," but rather, an "approach."

The ten principles that follow are intended as a summary of Buber's personalistic ethics. They are taken from these works: *Between Man and Man*,[20] *Eclipse of God*,[21] *I and Thou*,[22] and *Pointing the Way*.[24]

1. **The locus of truth is not to be found as the content of knowledge, but only as human existence.**

   Given that ethics is grounded in truth, where is the locus of truth? The four ethical systems being examined provide different answers. End-result ethics tells us that truth is found in consequences. Rule ethics contends that truth is found in universally valid laws. Social contract ethics would have us believe that truth is found in the customs and norms of a given community. Now, with personalistic ethics, we have a radical shift in the locus of truth. Rather than truth being "out there"—in consequences, laws, or community norms—it is "in here." That is, truth lies *within* each individual, and not merely within knowledge and intellect, but within the total person.

2. **Conscience is the voice that calls you to fulfill the personal intention of your being—of what you are intended to be—and thereby distinguishes and decides between right and wrong.**

   Given that truth lies within each individual, it then follows that the standards for moral conduct also must lie within the individual. Here is found the moral compass that provides direction for distinguishing between right and wrong. The consequence of straying from the compass is a feeling of guilt: "His conscience smites him." There are two types of individuals who seldom if ever feel guilty. The first are those who do not stray from their moral compasses. And the second are those who have no moral compasses. Other than not suffering from the pangs of conscience, there is no similarity between these two types of individuals.

3. **Your personal convictions should serve as the ultimate standard for determining what you should do.**
   Consistent with the different views of truth, each of the four

ethical systems proposes a different ultimate standard for determining what we should do. End-result ethics tells us that the ultimate standard is in expected consequences. Rule ethics contends that it is in laws and rules. Social contract ethics says that it is in the customs and norms of the community. Personalistic ethics now brings us back to ourselves: in the final analysis, it is our own personal convictions that should serve as the ultimate standard for determining what we should do.

4. **You must confront each situation and do that which is in keeping with it — with all that you are and know.**

A situation confronts you, and you must respond. You must respond with your total being, your total self as a fully functioning human being. As Buber would say, "When a situation accosts one, then that is not the time to consult a rule book." Indeed, it is up to you to decide what is right and what is wrong in this particular situation and at this particular time — and then act accordingly.

5. **If you take a road that in its nature does not already represent the nature of the goal, you will miss the goal. The goal that you reach will resemble the road you have reached it by.**

This principle should be read carefully and reflected upon. Here is where Buber expresses profound disagreement with end-result ethics insofar as it contends, in true Machiavellian fashion, that the end justifies the means. The individual who has a noble goal but employs an ignoble means to achieve the goal will surely miss the goal. Buber would stress, and rightly so, that this individual will end up achieving not a noble goal, but an ignoble goal. Whenever we try to justify an unethical action on the basis of its serving an ethical end, we are kidding ourselves. We must be reminded that the nature of the goal and the nature of the way must be in harmony.

6. **There are no absolute formulas for living — no preconceived code can see ahead to everything that can happen in your life.**

With this principle, Buber takes his stand against rule ethics. Kant contends that there are universally valid moral laws that apply to all human beings. And Kant stresses that it is one's *duty* to abide by these laws. Buber takes exception. He contends, for example, that even the commandment to honor your father and mother — for the child of an evil parent — may be impossible to uphold. Under these conditions, if the child is unable to live by the commandment, would you judge the child to be immoral?

7. **You must be able to be an active member of your group, but you must not let this prevent you from standing up for what is right.**

This principle brings into focus the distinction between Buber's personalistic ethics and Rousseau's social contract ethics. In the case of the latter, the individual is expected to submerge his or her individuality into the general will for the purpose of satisfying the common good. In the case of the former, the individual is expected to be an integral part of the community — *but still maintain his or her individuality.* Thus, if the individual disagrees with the community on an issue pertaining to right and wrong, he or she has a responsibility to "stand up and be heard." Stated differently, should the individual believe that the collective conscience is misdirected, then he or she should not stand by idly, but should endeavor to redirect it. It is here that we are able to see the clear distinction between the other-directed person and the inner-directed person, as well as between the blind follower and the responsible leader.

8. **As we "become free," this leaning on something is more and more denied to us, and our responsibility must become personal and solitary.**

Buber is placing in center stage the person who has achieved the level of Existenz, authentic selfhood. This person has moved from potential Existenz to *actual* Existenz. To some, this level of existence is unsettling, because previously held notions of morality may be brought into question. At the level of empirical existence, one had an understanding of pleasure and pain that provided direction. At the level of consciousness at large, one had universally valid laws to provide certainty. And at the level of spirit, one had the beliefs and values of the community to provide a sense of identity and belongingness. At each of these levels, the standards of right and wrong could be ascertained. (If in doubt, one could always ask others.) But now, at the level of Ex-

istenz, the individual does not have a great deal of external support to lean on — because the ultimate standards of morality now
come from within.

9. You can perfect yourself only in your own way and not in that of any other.

Buber stresses that every person born into this world
represents something new, something that never existed before,
something original and unique. Therefore, it is each person's
primary task to actualize his or her unique potentialities, and
not something that another has achieved. And so each person
has this opportunity and challenge: be yourself. Do not cling
to the rung of another; find your own rung and cultivate that
rung. Be yourself in your uniqueness, and be the best that you
can possibly be.

10. As we live, we must grow, and our beliefs change. They must change.

As the individual advances from one level of being to the
next — throughout a lifetime — we note changes in beliefs. At the
level of empirical existence, the infant learns very quickly that
crying will get results — in the form of a warm bottle of milk.
Next, at the level of consciousness at large, the child learns basic
rules of conduct that are viewed as absolute and go unquestioned.
Then, at the level of spirit, the teenager is confronted with com-
peting beliefs of the church, the home, and the peer group, and
must endeavor to reconcile them. Finally, moving toward the
level of Existenz, the mature adult realizes that, while the past
beliefs may have been of value, he or she must now forge a personally satisfying set of beliefs — from within. If such a process
of maturation does not unfold, the individual becomes completely
stuck at a lower level of being, and, at best, will be guided only
by partial maps, or segments of maps.

This brief summary cannot do justice to the breadth and richness
of Buber's works dealing with personalistic ethics. Nevertheless, it
should provide a general orientation to personalistic ethics and how
this approach differs from the others.

If we evaluate Buber's personalistic ethics on the basis of the quality of Buber's writings and the quality of his lived life, we must con

clude that it is truly remarkable. This approach to ethics was elucidated by a philosopher who perfected — or came very close to
perfecting — both his works and his life. He did not sacrifice one for
the other. How rare! But if we evaluate personalistic ethics in terms
of its usefulness to an organization, we may have some reservations.
Indeed, there are several fundamental questions that must be
addressed.

**How could we justify our actions except by saying, "Well, it felt
like the right thing for me to do"?** Consider a hypothetical case in
which you, as a vice president of a commercial bank, have a serious
problem with one of your young account managers. You have just
been informed that Carlos has insulted one of your major clients,
and the client is withdrawing her account from your bank. Upon
probing the matter with Carlos, you learn that he and the client
disagreed on what Carlos considered to be an ethical issue, and he
questioned the ethics of the client. (By the way, when you interviewed
Carlos for the job, you assured him that you were looking for independent thinkers who could "stand on their own feet.") You ask
Carlos if he had considered the consequences of his action? "Not
really." You next ask if he was acting in accordance with the written
policies and procedures of the bank. "I don't know." You then ask
if his actions were consistant with the underlying values of the
bank — and especially the one pertaining to customer satisfaction.
"Perhaps not." In a state of exasperation, you finally ask your young
account manager why he did what he did. He responds with conviction: "According to my own personal code of ethics, it felt like the
right thing to do." What would you do next?

How could we resolve conflicting views of two different persons?
You met with Carlos from 8:00 a.m. to 9:00 a.m. It is now 10:00 a.m.,
and you have been notified by your secretary that a second problem
needs your immediate attention. Two of your direct reports, James
and Julie, need to see you immediately. These are two of your best
people: as systems analysts, they are creative problem solvers who
get the job done. But they, as Carlos, are committed to personalistic
ethics. You invite the two systems analysts into your office and realize
immediately that tempers are flaring. After getting the two of them
to calm down, you learn that they are at complete odds on a matter
that they both deem to be an ethical issue. Being a good mediator,
you first ask James to express his views on the matter without allowing Julie to interrupt. Next, you ask Julie to do likewise. From these

expressions of viewpoints, it is clear to you that *each has a valid point in terms of his or her own code of ethics.* But the two are 180° apart! What would you do next?

What would be the common bond in a team that fostered personalistic ethics? During the lunch hour, as you are sitting in your office reflecting on the problems of the morning, your secretary comes in to remind you of your 1:00 p.m. meeting. As project director, you will be meeting with the newly established team that will carry out the system upgrade project. Because this is the bank's most important project of the year, the president has asked you, a vice president, to devote at least 50 percent of your time over the next 12 months to head up the project. The purpose of this initial meeting is to review several items, including project goals, work breakdown structure, schedules, budgets, assignments, and operational ground rules. When you begin reviewing the ground rules with the eight team members — all commited to personalistic ethics — the discussion becomes heated. During the ensuing discussion and debate, it becomes clear to you that these eight independent thinkers are poles apart in values and ethics. *And each is convinced that he or she is right.* As project director, what would you do to establish a common set of ground rules — pertaining to values and ethics — that all eight team members can live with?

How could an organization assure uniformity in ethics if it promoted personalistic ethics? It is now 5:30 p.m. You have had a pretty rough day and decide to head for home. As you walk past the president's office, he asks you to come in. The president is just beginning to draft a code of ethics for the bank, and he wants your ideas on one particular matter. If the code of ethics is to establish a set of common ethical standards for all of the bank's employees, what is the role of personalistic ethics? The president has become aware of the notion of personalistic ethics through his recent discussions with several of the bank's youngest professionals who have taken an ethics course as part of their M.B.A. program. He can appreciate how personalistic ethics might be used in one's personal life, but he doesn't understand how such an individualistic approach to ethics might fit into a code of ethics for an organization. He wants your counsel. What would you tell him?

The purpose of these hypothetical cases is not to disparage Martin Buber's personalistic ethics but, rather, to bring into question those persons who attempt to apply personalistic ethics *without regard for other ethical systems.*

It is important to appreciate that Buber himself was exemplary in living out of the Encompassing. He was guided principally by Existenz, but he was very much at home in the domains of empirical existence, consciousness at large, and spirit. There are others, however, who want to achieve the level of Existenz by bypassing the first three levels. Rather than "authentic Existenz," we call this "pseudo Existenz."

In a similar vein, Buber was exemplary in the practice of personalistic ethics. He was guided principally by his conscience, but was cognizant of the importance of expected consequences, rules, and the customs and norms of a given community. But the individuals living at the level of pseudo Existenz want to follow only their consciences, while ignoring expected consequences, rules, and the customs and norms of the community. These individuals are on shaky ground.

We will end this review of personalistic ethics with a nautical metaphor. The four modes of being are to be depicted as a ship and a rudder. Represented by the ship are three levels of being—empirical existence, consciousness at large, and spirit. Represented by the rudder is Existenz. Buber's life is reflected clearly by both the ship and the rudder. But the individual who attempts to live at the level of Existenz while bypassing the other levels—or to be guided by conscience while ignoring expected consequences, rules, and customs and norms—is like a rudder without a ship.

SUMMING UP

In summing up this chapter on ethical systems, it is appropriate to return now to the quotation by Father Hesburgh:

> My basic principle is that you don't make decisions because they are easy, you don't make them because they are cheap, you don't make them because they are popular; you make them because they are right.[53, p.172]

We then raised the question: How does one go about determining what is "right"? In other words, what ground rules should a person follow in deciding what is right and what is wrong? In seeking an answer, we have reviewed four markedly different approaches to ethics—end-result ethics, rule ethics, social contract ethics, and personalistic ethics.

Note that each of these four different view of ethics has a different locus of authority. With end-result ethics, the locus of authority is in *expected consequences*. With rule ethics, it is found in *laws* and *standards*. With social contract ethics, it is in the *customs* and *norms* of the community or society. And with personalistic ethics, the locus of authority is found in one's *conscience*.

Consider how these grounds of authority might apply to real people in the everyday world. For illustrative purposes, we can focus on the Golden Rule: "Do unto others as you would have them do unto you." Taking a specific case, we will assume that someone has been asked by a co-worker for a ride to work the following morning (which will mean an additional 20 minutes of driving both to and from work). How might the person respond to the request under each of the four ethical systems? These might be the thought processes:

- Under end-result ethics: "I probably should do it because I may want her to give me a ride at some later date."
- Under rule ethics: "I will do it because this is what the Golden Rule tells me to do, and I always follow the Golden Rule."
- Under social contract ethics: "I find this somewhat inconvenient, but it seems the proper thing to do according to company policy."
- Under personalistic ethics: "I will do it because it is the right thing for someone like me to do."

It could be argued that each one of these four individuals is being guided by the Golden Rule — but under completely different ground rules.

In the light of these illustrations, we can now see (as shown in Figure 17) how the four ethical systems are aligned with the four modes of being. A person who is limited to the level of empirical existence would tend toward end-result ethics. A person who has moved to consciousness at large would tend toward rule ethics. One who has advanced to the level of spirit probably would be committed to social contract ethics. And the person who has achieved Existenz more than likely would be at home with personalistic ethics. (It is interesting to speculate that the philosopher who first proposed a particular ethical system must have been functioning at the corresponding level of being. And if this is not the case, then he must have believed that the rest of humanity should function at that particular level.)

The pros and cons of each of these four ethical systems have been

LEVELS OF BEING	ETHICAL SYSTEMS
Empirical Existence	End-result Ethics
Consciousness at Large	Rule Ethics
Spirit	Social Contract Ethics
Existenz	Personalistic Ethics

Figure 17.   Relation between levels of being and ethical systems.

debated by the philosophers of ethics ad infinitum. Such debates are problematic. Viewed in the light of the Encompassing, it is seen that each ethical system is linked to a different mode of being. And just as no single mode of being constitutes the whole, no one of the four ethical systems constitutes the whole. But each can make a contribution to the whole. In the vernacular of "maps," we can say that each of these four systems of ethics represents only a partial map of the good life, but even so, can serve as an integral part of the total map.

The promise of a comprehensive map of the good life is found in the Encompassing. While the Encompassing will provide no definitive answers to specific ethical questions, it nevertheless will provide a framework for structuring our thinking about ethical issues.

1. The proposed theory of ethics is a comprehensive map of the good life, a life worth living.
2. The map has two sides — each a mirror of the other.
3. One side represents a comprehensive view of the good life in the form of four levels of being — empirical existence, consciousness at large, spirit, and Existenz — all being connected by the bond of reason.

4. The second side represents a comprehensive view of ethics in the form of four levels of ethics — end-result ethics, rule ethics, social contract ethics, and personalistic ethics — all being connected by the bond of reason.

5. And the principal feature of the map is that it has *integrity:* "As a synthesizing form of thought, integrity acts to *preserve the whole* by accepting polarities, appreciating differences, and finding connections that transcend and encompass all points of view."

6. We may then conclude that the truly ethical person is one who finds his or her way in life by use of the total map — i.e., lives out of the Encompassing.

We may now ask: How would such a theory work in everyday life?

Let's suppose that I am faced with a serious ethical dilemma — one in which I must choose between two alternative courses of action. How might I approach the problem? The diagram in Figure 18 displays my strategy.

First, I would consider the likely consequences associated with each of the two alternatives (end-result ethics). Next, I would review any laws or rules that might apply to this particular situation (rule

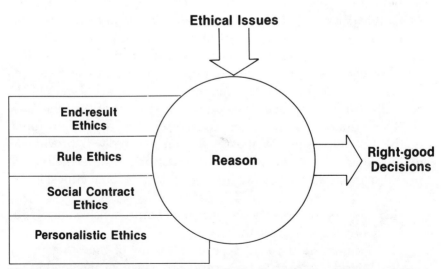

This diagram is an adaptation of one used in the Leadership Core Curriculum of the Advanced Officer Course (Lesson 3: Professional Ethics) for the U.S. Army and the U.S. Military Academy at West Point.

Figure 18.   An Encompassing theory of ethics.

ethics). Then next, I would consider the norms and customs of the particular organization/community/society within which I am taking action (social contract ethics). Then finally, I would reflect on my personal convictions regarding the matter (personalistic ethics).

Running through all of these steps is my active reasoning process: clearly defining the problem, viewing the problem in its entirety, analyzing the parts successively, and then making a decision. Most important, this will be a decision that I will be able to defend — both to myself and to others — and will be one that I can live with.

We then ask: What was the principal criterion on which the decision was decided? Was it expected consequences? Was it a given law or rule? Was it the customs or norms of the organization/community/society within which I was operating? Or was it simply my conscience? The answer is that it was none of these per se, yet it was all of these. Essentially, it was my reason that served as the final arbiter.

Does this mean, then, that one's reason can override one's conscience? Heavy stuff here, but this is true. The open-minded person, when faced with a situation as the above and being committed to making a right-good decision through the use of reason, *will alter convictions previously held*. Otherwise, how would the person ever grow?

Thus, we are now in a much better position to understand the role of each of the four ethical systems. Further, we can now understand why the numerous debates pitting one system against another have been pointless: *because each ethical system reflects a different mode of being.* Inasmuch as each mode of being has its own form of truth, each ethical system also has its own form of truth. Thus, we can conclude that each ethical system can make a unique contribution to the whole. It is as though the cataracts had been removed from our eyes.

With this brief overview of an Encompassing theory of ethics, we now turn to the link between ethics and leadership styles.

V

Leadership Styles

In management, as in music, there is a base clef as well
as a treble. The treble generally carries the melody in music,
and melody's equivalent in management is the manager's
style. A manager's style — the way he focuses his attention
and interacts with people — sets the "tune" for his subordinates and communicates at the operational level what his
expectations are and how he wants business conducted.

Richard Pascale and Anthony Athos
The Art of Japanese Management[97, p.177]

The Importance of Leadership • *The Manipulator* • *The Bureaucratic
Administrator* • *The Professional Manager* • *The Transforming Leader* •
Summing Up

THE IMPORTANCE OF LEADERSHIP

As chairman of RCA, Thornton Bradshaw has a clear understanding
of the importance of moral leadership. He offers to each and every
manager these words of wisdom:

> I'm a great believer that leadership, in a large part, is moral
> leadership. And people want to follow moral leadership.
> They respect it. And they expect it too. That's not being
> specific, but if the head of a business, for instance, ac-
> complishes everything the shareholders want in terms of in-
> creasing the price of shares and increasing dividends and
> earnings and so forth — if he still fails in terms of this moral

135

> leadership, in the long run, that company is not going to
> prosper.[39. p.227]

Bradshaw is making reference here to the chief executive officer,
the individual who establishes the overall climate for the organization as a whole. But the statement is applicable to every manager
in the organization, from the chief executive down to the first-level
supervisor.

The world of business would be a different world if managers
would understand the profound impact of their behavior on the
ethical conduct of their people. Through their words, actions, and
even body language, managers do indeed influence the ethical conduct of their people. Granted, each employee's ethics is influenced
by upbringing and past experience. But, now as an adult, the person's ethical conduct has no small amount of elasticity—in other
words, it is not a constant, but a variable. The degree to which this
conduct varies on an ethics continuum either from low to high or
from high to low is influenced greatly by the employee's superiors.

The importance of the manager's behavior in influencing the
ethical conduct of employees is brought into focus by Schmidt and
Posner.[110] As shown in Figure 19, of the five primary factors that influence ethical conduct in organizations, the behavior of superiors
was ranked first. This was followed, in order, by behavior of peers
in the organization, ethical practices of one's industry or profession,

Rank	
1	Behavior of superiors
2	Behavior of one's peers in the organization
3	Ethical practices of one's industry or profession
4	Society's moral climate
5	Existence of formal organizational policy

Schmidt and Posner: *Managerial Values in Perspective*, p. 35

Figure 19. Determinants of ethical behavior in organizations.

society's moral climate, and existence of formal organizational policy.

The ethical situation in organizations may be likened to a spaceship heading directly toward a distant planet. The destination represents the focus on achieving clearly defined objectives. The structure of the capsule represents the particular laws and rules that must not be violated. But what happens within the spaceship throughout the long journey is determined essentially by the commander and deputy commanders. The commanders establish a social climate that communicates to the crew the ground rules—"the way we do things around here." And the crew members won't miss a beat.

We want to examine the relation between ethics and the behavior of managers. There are numerous books that describe different ethical systems, and there are large numbers of books that describe different leadership styles. Of primary interest here is the connection between the ethical systems and the leadership styles.

We can identify four particular leadership styles that correspond to the four ethical systems described in the previous chapter. The four types of leaders can be defined in terms of how they view their primary function:

- **Manipulator.** The primary function of leadership is to use deception and cunning to further one's own ends. (The end justifies the means.)
- **Bureaucratic administrator.** The primary function of leadership is to communicate and enforce rules. (Structure is preserved through rules.)
- **Professional manager.** The primary function of leadership is to get things done through people for the purpose of achieving organizational objectives. (Management is grounded in the responsibility for achieving results through the effective and efficient use of human and material resources.)
- **Transforming leader.** The primary function of leadership is to lift followers to their better selves. (The most effective way to motivate is to bring out the best in others.)

These four very different leadership styles are aligned with the four ethical systems as shown in Figure 20. End-result ethics leads to manipulation; rule ethics bring about bureaucratic administration; social contract ethics promotes professional management; and personalistic ethics results in transforming leadership. This is a reasonably good alignment—not perfect, but reasonably good. What the alignment tells us is that, if a particular manager has made a

ETHICAL SYSTEMS	LEADERSHIP STYLES
End-result Ethics	Manipulator
Rule Ethics	Bureaucratic Administrator
Social Contract Ethics	Professional Manager
Personalistic Ethics	Transforming Leader

Figure 20.   Relation between ethical systems and leadership styles.

genuine commitment to one of the four ethical systems, the probability is rather high that he or she will manifest the corresponding leadership style. (This assumes, of course, that the manager has freedom in the choice of leadership style.)

Every manager should benefit from an understanding of the four ethical systems and the four leadership styles — and the connection between the two. This understanding should lead to an examination of one's own ethics and leadership style, as well as the likely effects on others. If taken seriously, even unsettling insights can be beneficial. As the Greek sage told us, "The first step to wisdom is to know thyself."

To this end, I hope that you will study carefully the four leadership styles presented on the following pages. They are intended to serve as a mirror for you. If you do not like what you see, perhaps you should consider making some adjustments in your leadership style. Making such changes in a positive and constructive manner constitutes learning at its very best.

THE MANIPULATOR

> For over four hundred years, *The Prince* has been the basic
> handbook of politics, statesmanship, and power. Written
> by a Florentine nobleman whose name has become a
> synonym for crafty plotting, it is a fascinating political and
> social document, as pertinent today as when it first ap-
> peared. Machiavelli wanted to set down for all time the
> rules and moves in the ageless game of politics, and, as the
> most successful statesman of his day, he devised this highly
> readable formula for the person who seeks power. There
> was little modern democracy in sixteenth century Italy, and
> as a result, Machiavelli's work became thought of as a
> blueprint for dictators — instead of a guide for efficient
> democratic government. [77, p.i]

And so begins the preface to a modern-day edition of Machiavelli's
classic book, *The Prince*, one of the most popular books in western
civilization. Published in 1537, it is readily available in paperback
in many book stores today.

The Prince contains a wealth of advice on how to survive (from
Machiavelli to Prince Lorenzo the Magnificent of Florence). In earlier
days, the book was studied by such kings and ministers as Richelieu,
Christina of Sweden, Frederick of Prussia, Bismarck, and Clem-
enceau. In the twentieth century, the book influenced national leaders
such as Mussolini, Hitler, Lenin, and Stalin.

Even with this questionable circle of followers, it is evident today that Machiavellianism is alive and thriving. Among no small
number of managers, the basic strategy of manipulating others to
further one's own ends is considered standard operating procedure.

The keystone of Machiavelli's philosophy of leadership and power
is found in this passage:

> The end justifies the means. Let a prince therefore aim at
> conquering and maintaining the state, and the means will
> always be judged as honourable and praised by every
> one. [77, p.94]

The underlying premise of Machiavellianism is that the end
justifies the means. And the "end" refers to your own end, not that
of others. Whatever you need to do to achieve the end is
permissible — just so long as you are successful in achieving the end.
In the final analysis, you will be judged not on how you achieved
the end, but whether or not you achieved it. (It will be to your ad-

vantage, of course, to endeavor to operate within the law, because otherwise you may not be able to achieve your end.)

It is disturbing to me to note the large number of recent books on management that are grounded in Machiavellianism — and become "best sellers." Typically, the theme of such works is "This is how I made it to the top (or made my first million dollars), and you can do it too. Just follow these steps."

"Power and the Ambitious Executive," a paper published by Robert McMurry[87] in 1973, could have been titled "Machiavellianism in Practice." Not only was the paper published by *Harvard Business Review*, a leading management journal, but it was selected by the HBR editors as one of the reprints in a book of readings on leadership.

What follows in the form of ten principles of manipulative leadership is taken from McMurry's paper. It would be difficult to find a more succinct statement of Machiavellianism — or what might be called "the art of being an effective manipulator."

1. **The most important requirement for success in an organization is *power*.** *

   Throughout your career as a manager, your basic strategy for success should be to gain as much power as possible — to be able to control people and events. Of the three basic human needs — achievement, affiliation, and power — the last is of utmost importance for success in management. Push the other two needs into the background and concentrate on power.

   You should actively cultivate three basic sources of power — information, resources, and support. Information includes knowledge of your particular field, knowledge of what is happening within the organization, and knowledge of the external environment insofar as it may have some impact on the organization. Resources include staff, equipment, facilities, and money. And support includes the endorsement of upper management, your people, and your peers. All three of these sources of power should be developed in a concentrated and systematic fashion.

   Remember: the most important requirement for your success in management is *power*.

---

*Throughout the chapter, the statement of principle in boldface type is taken almost verbatim from the identified author, but the elaboration of the principle is my own.

2. **Power is the capacity to modify the conduct of others in a desired manner, together with the capacity to avoid having one's own behavior modified in undesired ways by others.**

   You should make every effort to control others and prevent them from controlling you. The catchword is "always have the upper hand."

   To this end, there is a basic strategy that guarantees success. We will call it the "mini-max" strategy. The idea is to *minimize* the amount of information the other person obtains about you while you *maximize* the amount of information you obtain about the other person. The way to go about this is to probe and probe to get to the inner core of the other person's basic personality makeup — to find out what makes the person "tick." This will help you determine "what button to push." In turn, you should reveal only a facade of your own inner self and never, never allow the other person to penetrate this facade. The key is to be ever-vigilant.

3. **Without power, there can be no authority; without authority, there can be no discipline; without discipline, there can be difficulty in maintaining order, system, and productivity.**

   As you move up the management ladder, you will be given increasing amounts of responsibility. Throughout this career advancement, it is important that you always have an amount of authority that equals — or even exceeds — the level of responsibility. To be able to control others, you must endeavor to maximize your authority.

   To this end, always move toward those jobs that hold the most authority. For example, if a line position such as department manager promises a considerable amount of authority, go for it. On the other hand, if a position such as program manager (which holds little formal authority) opens up for you, avoid it like a plague. Then, once in a new position, do whatever you can to expand the amount of authority for that particular position.

4. **You should recognize the power of the purse — and position yourself so that you approve all budgets.**

   Financial resources are needed by all managers. And in most

organizations, financial resources are a scarce commodity. Thus, the manager who has control over this scarce commodity has considerable power over others.

Whatever your level of management in the organization, make certain that the approval of budgets rests only with you. If there are managers two or three levels below you, it should be made known to all of them that the sole authority for the approval of budgets is you. This understanding among the subordinate managers should lead them to solicit your favor and approval not only during the budget review period, but throughout the entire year.

5. **In business, as in diplomacy, the most important strategem of power is to establish alliances.**

For you to achieve your goals and advance in the organization, you will need the support of others. While the Lone Ranger may have been successful in his particular environment, he would have encountered great difficulty as a manager in a formal organization. You cannot afford to be a Lone Ranger. Establish your alliances.

The key to success will be to identify those individuals throughout the organization who have the most power. You will not be able to do this simply from a review of the organization charts. And further, you should realize that a particular manager who has considerable power today may have very little tomorrow — even though that manager carries the same job title. Thus, it requires a considerable amount of continual probing to ascertain who are the actual power wielders at any given time.

Once you have identified the individuals who hold the most power, develop a plan for systematically cultivating these individuals. Then implement the plan!

6. **One good means of ensuring support from peers is to identify common goals and a common enemy.**

Once you have decided upon those individuals with whom you want to ally yourself, get busy in cultivating their support. You want to do two things: (1) identify common goals and (2) identify a common enemy.

For any alliance to work, both parties must stand to benefit from the relationship. A one-way contribution will not endure. By identifying common goals, it will become clear how the relationship will be mutually beneficial. The synergy generated from the joint effort should place both you and your ally in a better position to achieve your goals.

But you need more than this commitment to common goals, which is only conceptual. In addition, there must be a psychological bonding. This can best be achieved by identifying a common enemy — be it a particular manager in the organization or a particular department. A rewarding way to spend your lunch hours is with your ally commiserating about this common enemy. You will then be wedded both intellectually and emotionally.

7. **Because many employees resent discipline and seek "happiness" as their ultimate goal, it is essential that you have power to discipline these employees.**

The old adage "Spare the rod and spoil the child" applies equally to children and adults. It is true that, basically, people are lazy and irresponsible. Given this truth about human nature, it is essential that, to control the behavior of your subordinates, you have the power to apply punitive measures.

The key is to get control of the motivators. Make certain that you have these authorities: to either increase or decrease salaries, to promote and demote, to approve or disapprove all requests for education and training, and to approve or disapprove all purchase requests. Then use these motivators to achieve your own ends. It will be to your advantage if your subordinates clearly understand that you control both the carrot and stick — it will keep them "on their toes."

8. **You should seek subordinates who not only have the requisite technical skills but who are also to some degree passive, dependent, and submissive.**

In selecting new employees, you should seek people who have the knowledge and skills to do the job. This information should be readily available from the resumé, the references, and the interview. But just as important as the knowledge and skills required — and perhaps even more important — is the trait of submissiveness.

You want employees who are controllable. The type of employee who is a free thinker and who questions your decisions is disruptive and will only frustrate you in your efforts to succeed. If, perchance, you happen to obtain such an employee, take corrective action by removing the individual from your unit immediately. Try to minimize such mistakes! Through in-depth interviewing and scrutiny of body language, you should be able to spot those candidates who are passive, dependent, and submissive. If they have the requisite technical skills, hire them.

9. **You should radiate self-confidence by giving the impression that you know what you are doing and are completely in command of the situation, even though you may not be sure at all.**

You should always act as though you are in complete command of every situation. This demeanor will generate confidence in your subordinates, admiration from your superiors, and fear in your adversaries.

It is essential that you learn how to "wing it." There is no way possible for you to be on top of all the facts at all times. But you can act as though you have a complete grasp of all the facts. To this end, always stay abreast of the "big picture" and the key issues facing the organization. As long as you are aware of the broad issues, you can then convey the impression of complete comprehension. For example, in response to a question (raised in a group meeting) for which you do not have a ready answer, you might reply, "I had assumed that you were interested in the broader ramifications of the problem. But if you are interested in micro-managing, I will have my administrative assistant send you the detailed figures." Stay in command!

10. **You should maintain maneuverability by never committing yourself completely and irrevocably — so that you can always change without loss of face.**

The message here is to never get backed into a corner: be sure that you always have an "out." Even though you will inevitably suffer some setbacks, it is important that you never *appear* to have failed.

The following example illustrates how this principle might be applied. Suppose that you are responsible for managing a large project that is of considerable importance to the organization. At the outset, make certain that the project has *several* goals. Once the project is completed, you may find that some of the goals were not achieved. Don't retreat! Certainly, you achieved at least *one* of the goals. Then, when you write the final report, slant it in such a way to indicate that the goal you achieved was in fact the *primary* goal, and the others were secondary and even tertiary. So indeed you did achieve the primary goal. Always maintain maneuverability. Stay in command!

Let's return now to the grand master of manipulation, Machiavelli, who offers these words of advice:

> It is not necessary for a prince to have all of the above-named qualities, but it is very necessary to *seem* to have them. I would even be bold to say that to possess them and always to observe them is dangerous, but to *appear* to possess them is useful. Thus it is well to seem merciful, faithful, humane, sincere, religious, and able to be so; but you must have the mind so disposed that when it is needful to be otherwise you may be able to change to the opposite qualities.[77, p.93]

Now tell me, dear reader, how would you like to work for a manager who lived by this Machiavellian philosophy? Perhaps your answer is, "But I do." Such a reply would not be surprising, because manipulative managers, unfortunately, are plentiful.

We then move to this question: What is the relation between Machiavellianism and ethics? We can witness a clear-cut chain of causal relations. The pure Machiavellian manager is living at the level of empirical existence, the bottom rung of the Encompassing ladder. As a consequence of being stuck at this level of being, the leader embraces end-result ethics, convinced that the end justifies the means. The only thing that counts is the achievement of results; *how* the results are achieved does not matter.

What it all boils down to is that end-result ethics in the form of Machiavellianism can best be described as "missing ethics." But it is important to note that leaders who are restricted to this domain are not necessarily immoral. Rather, they are amoral — which means that ethics and morality are simply not part of their lives. Very much present are the economic dimension and the egoistic dimension, but missing is the ethics dimension.

The principal consequence of Machiavellian leadership is that it leads to lack of trust. Without trust, there can be no genuine relationship between leader and follower. And without a genuine relationship between leader and follower, there can be no effective leadership. We may very well find short-term gains but long-term disasters. Thus, we must conclude that there is a better leadership style.

THE BUREAUCRATIC ADMINISTRATOR

It was Max Weber, the renowned German sociologist, who elucidated a form of leadership that stood as a polar opposite to Machiavellianism. As an astute observer of organizations, Weber saw the emergence of a type of leadership that would rationalize the leadership function—would make it conformable to rational principles.

Writing at the turn of this century, Weber highlighted a basic flaw in the common leadership styles that had prevailed throughout history. With patriarchalism, the leader was the founder or oldest member of the group. With patrimonialism, the leadership role was inherited from one's father or other ancestor. With feudalism, it was the lord over the vassal. In all of these forms of leadership, the power and authority of leadership was centered in a single individual. What inevitably happened whenever such a leader either died or was deposed of was that the collective body under the leader's command suffered from confusion and uncertainty—and perhaps chaos—until another such leader emerged to take command and bring order.

Weber highlighted the need for a type of organizational structure that transcended the individual leader. Organizations needed stability and endurance, which would be impossible to achieve through any of the previously mentioned leadership styles. Organizations needed a type of structure and management that would provide staying power, that would allow them to continue to function *regardless of what happened to the individual leader.*

The solution to the problem was found in bureaucracy. Today, the term "bureaucracy" carries a great deal of negative connotation, suggesting red tape and petty officiating. But we must appreciate that, at the time of Weber's writing, a bureaucratic structure promised an approach that would cure the dominant leadership styles of their ills. And we can surely appreciate that, in many quarters today, bureaucracy continues to thrive.

The essence of bureaucracy is captured by Weber in this passage:

> The management of the office follows general rules, which are more or less stable, more or less exhaustive, and which can be learned. Knowledge of these rules represents a special technical learning which the officials possess. . . .
> The reduction of modern office management to rules is deeply embedded in the very nature of bureaucracy.[44, p.198]

We can see that, with this view of management, the locus of

authority has shifted dramatically from the individual leader to the governing rules. The establishment of such a system of management would mean that the members of an organization would no longer be subject to the whims of a capricious leader, but would be guided in their conduct by stable rules. Capriciousness and irrationality would be replaced by stability and rationality. Indeed, how simple it seems: to reduce modern office management to rules.

What follows is a set of principles underlying bureaucratic administration. These principles are drawn from Weber's essays on bureaucracy, included in the book *From Max Weber: Essays in Sociology*, edited by Gerth and Mills.[44]

As you read these principles of bureaucracy, think about the various organizations with which you are familiar, and consider which of these organizations (if any) abide by all or most of the principles.

1. **The organization should be arranged in a hierarchy of offices, with each office under the control and supervision of the next highest.**

   The root word of organization is "organic"—meaning the elements "fit together into a unified whole." This is what organization is about: all of the elements are tied together in a functional whole.

   To achieve the coordination needed for efficient functioning, an organization needs structure. And the best way to achieve structure is through a hierarchy of offices. At the top of the hierarchy is the director of the organization, next are the deputy directors, and so on down to the bottom of the hierarchy.

   Such a structure clarifies the authority of each position in the organization and who has authority over whom. The defined organizational structure should be presented in an organizational chart and made available to all members of the organization.

2. **Every position in the organization should have a clearly prescribed job description—a fixed route of march.**

   Each person in the organization needs a clear set of duties set forth in a written job description that encompasses all of the essential elements of the job. This would include job mission, principal functions, and specific responsibilities. Further, it should clearly specify the type of authority or level of authority for the position.

Upon being assigned to a new position, the job incumbent should receive a job description for the position and an orientation by the immediate supervisor. It should be made clear to the job incumbent that he or she will be held accountable for everything included in the job description. This is the "fixed route of march."

3. **The organization should be governed by rules that are fixed, more or less exhaustive, and capable of being learned.**

To assure that each employee follows the "fixed route of march," it is essential that the organization have a comprehensive set of rules — regulations governing employee conduct. Rules are the means of assuring that all employees are marching to the same drummer.

The rules should be exhaustive: they should cover all common situations as well as every possible contingency. They should specify what type of behavior is expected and what type of behavior is unacceptable. Further, they should clearly specify the consequences or punitive measures associated with unacceptable behavior.

The rules should be included in an operations manual that is made available to every person in a managerial or supervisory position. Importantly, the operations manual should be written in such a manner to reduce ambiguity and to minimize the need for reflection and deliberation. To this end, the rules should be written at a level that can be comprehended by the least educated individuals in the organization.

4. **The primary function of management is the communication and enforcement of rules.**

Why are managers needed in an organization? What is their "value added"? There is a pure and simple answer — to communicate and enforce rules.

The first duty of each manager is to learn the rules of the organization. Through intensive study of the operations manual and questioning of superiors for clarification, each manager should commit to memory the entire body of rules.

The second duty of each manager is to communicate the rules

to every subordinate under his or her command. This should be done immediately upon the hiring of a new employee. And then, as specific situations arise, the applicable rules should be communicated through memos and oral instructions.

Then finally, the third duty of each manager is to assure that the rules are enforced. Enforcement calls for punishment of transgressors. Without enforcement, rules are hollow.

5. **Managerial functions should be carried out according to calculable rules and without regard for persons.**

"Bureaucracy develops the more perfectly," notes Max Weber, "the more the bureaucracy is 'dehumanized,' the more completely it succeeds in eliminating from official business love, hatred, and all purely personal, irrational, and emotional elements which escape calculation. This is the specific nature of bureaucracy and it is appraised as its special virture."[44, p.216]

We stated at the outset that the purpose of bureaucracy is to rationalize the leadership function. This rationalization calls for structure, rules, and, above all, objectivity. Introducing the personal dimension into the equation would disrupt the entire process. Hence, it is essential that every manager make a special effort to totally eliminate all subjectivity and emotion from the management function. The catchword is "objectivity above all."

6. **Employees should be appointed on the basis of their technical qualifications and should not be subject to arbitrary terminations.**

A bureaucratic organization has no place for patronage. Giving jobs to friends or relatives — simply because they are friends or relatives — is completely contrary to the basic principles on which a bureaucratic organization is established. All appointments should be based purely on objective considerations of technical qualifications. To achieve this objectivity, the best means of selecting new employees is through written tests. All personnel selections should be based primarily on the test scores. This approach completely eliminates favoritism, subjectivity, and bias.

Once employees are in their jobs, they should not be subject to arbitrary terminations. When Henry Ford II was asked why he fired his vice president, Lee Iacocca, he replied: "I simply

don't like him." Such a reason for terminating an employee would
be unacceptable in a bureaucratic organization.

7. **A system of promotions should exist whereby an employee may advance by virtue of seniority, achievement, or both.**

A bureaucratic structure is a pyramid of interlinking job posi-
tions, with each position reporting to the next higher position,
until we get to the position of director. Most employees, in order
to achieve greater status and salary, will desire to advance in
the organization.

Promotions should be based upon two criteria. The first
criterion should be seniority: if several individuals are eligible
to be promoted to a particular position, the one who has been
in his or her present position the longest should be given preferential treatment. But consideration also should be give to achievement: if several individuals are eligible to be promoted to a particular position, the one who has demonstrated the greatest
loyalty to the organization and the ability to carry out the
prescribed functions with the least disruption to the organization should be given preferential treatment. Thus, seniority and
achievement should be the two principal criteria on which to
base promotions, and each organization must decide on the
relative weighting.

8. **Salary should be administered according to status or rank and length of service.**

It is essential that salary be administered in a completely objective manner, to prevent discontentment among the
employees — which would be counterproductive to the efficient
functioning of the organization.

Generally it is a simple matter to establish a salary scale on
the basis of a two-way table, with rank and seniority as the two
axes of the table and the corresponding salary levels in the cells
of the table. Such an approach to administering salaries is completely objective and should eliminate bias and favoritism.

9. **Employees should be subject to strict and systematic discipline and control in the conduct of their work.**

A bureaucratic organization is based upon structure, authority, and control. Lack of control will lead to lack of efficiency. And lack of efficiency will encumber the entire organization. Hence, all members must abide strictly by the rules of the organization. Deviations from the rules must be dealt with immediately and consistently.

An effective control system includes several essential features. First, the standards for proper employee conduct must be clearly delineated. Second, there must be a method for monitoring the actual conduct of employees. And third, any deviations between the actual conduct and the standards must be dealt with immediately. Importantly, minor deviations must be dealt with before they become major deviations.

10. **The organization should be firmly established as a mechanism so that it can continue to function efficiently even with a change of leadership.**

Leaders will come and go. Some will resign or retire, some will die in office, some will be deposed of, and others will be voted out of office. The important thing is that the organization continue to function efficiently *regardless of what happens to the leader.*

A bureaucratic organization has the properties of a mechanism — a mechanical operation that does not need a steersman. The mechanism known as bureaucracy will have the properties of structure, order, system, discipline, and rules. These features will assure that the organization has stability and ongoing efficiency — perhaps forever.

We will end our description of bureaucracy with this passage from Max Weber that highlights the principal advantages of a bureaucratic organization:

> The decisive reason for the advance of bureaucratic organization has always been its purely technical superiority over any other form of organization. The fully developed bureaucratic mechanism compares with other organizations exactly as does the machine with the non-mechanical modes of production. ... Precision, speed, unambiguity, knowledge of the files, continuity, discretion, unity, strict subordination, reduction of friction and of material and personal costs — these are raised to the optimum point in the strictly bureaucratic organization.[44, p.214]

Question: How would you like to work in an organization that is governed by these principles of bureaucracy? Perhaps your answer is, "But I do." Such a reply would not be surprising, because, in many quarters, bureaucracy is alive and well — it continues to thrive.

We then move to this question: What is the relation between bureaucratic administration and ethics? The answer will give us greater understanding of both bureaucracy and ethics.

To fully appreciate the relation between bureaucratic administration and ethics, we must consider two important links in the causal chain. The first is the relation between consciousness at large and rule ethics, and the second is the relation between rule ethics and bureaucratic administration.

Beginning with consciousness at large, recall that this is the second level of being in the Encompassing hierarchy. The focus here is on objective knowledge, that which is universally valid. This mode of being is associated with several basic values: evidence, facts, precision, clarity, demonstrability, verifiability, predictability, certainty, orderliness, and lawfulness. Consciousness at large can best be described as a scientific outlook on life.

Immanuel Kant applied this scientific outlook to the field of ethics. To Kant, there was little difference between the laws of ethics and the laws of science. Both can be laid down as basic rules that govern our lives.

Moving next from ethics to leadership style, the relation between rule ethics and bureaucratic administration is evident. They are both grounded in consciousness at large — the desire for objectivity, structure, and certainty. The manager who is completely stuck at the level of consciousness at large undoubtedly would choose — if given the choice — bureaucratic administration as his or her preferred leadership style. Here we see perfect compatibility.

As a manifestation of an ethical system, bureaucratic administration has both strengths and limitations. The strengths witnessed in such properties as structure, systems, and objectivity cannot be denied. But the weaknesses of this leadership style warrant our special consideration.

Consider, for example, an example of misguided bureaucratic administration (or rule ethics) reported in the Columbus *Dispatch* in 1987. On the front page of the newspaper was a picture of a mother and her young daughter standing in front of their home, which had been almost destroyed by a fire. The story reached the front page because the mailman had refused to give the mother her monthly welfare check, which she desperately needed. According to the article, the check was not delivered because the mail box had been destroyed by the fire. The rule states that all welfare checks must be deposited in mail boxes, and to complicate matters, the system does not allow the forwarding of welfare checks. The reason given by the postman for not delivering the check was that he was *simply following the rules*. No ambiguity here.

Going back in time to 1955, we can point to another example of misguided bureaucratic administration (or rule ethics). The setting was Montgomery, Alabama, where city buses are an essential means of public transportation. The drivers of these buses were governed by a number of rules, but there is one in particular that many will recall: BLACKS MUST SIT IN THE REAR OF THE BUS. It was each driver's duty to enforce the rule. When Rosa Parks refused to obey this rule, trouble erupted. It was Martin Luther King, Jr., the black civil rights leader, who came forth to exhort that the requirement for blacks to sit in the rear of the bus was a stupid rule. He stressed that there was a "higher law" than the one that governed bus passengers in Montgomery, Alabama. So here we witness a style of leadership that rises above that of bureaucratic administration. But that's a story we will deal with later.

THE PROFESSIONAL MANAGER

In making the transition from bureaucratic administration to professional management, it is important that we distinguish between two important concepts — efficiency and effectiveness. To be *efficient* means "to function in the best possible or least wasteful manner." To be *effective* means "to produce the intended or expected result." Stated differently, we can say that efficiency is "doing things right," and effectiveness is "doing the right things."

The distinction between efficiency and effectiveness points up one of the key differences between bureaucratic administration and professional management. Whereas bureaucratic administration focuses on efficiency, professional management focuses on effectiveness.

Focusing on the concept of effectiveness, Peter Drucker elucidated the roles and responsibilities of the professional manager. With more than a dozen books published on the subject of management, Drucker has given us a clear picture of the functions of the professional manager.

The central function of the professional manager is captured in this passage by Drucker:

> For management is the organ, the life-giving, acting, dynamic organ of the institution it manages. Without the institution, e.g., the business enterprise, there would be no management. But without management there would also be only a mob rather than an institution. The institution, in turn, is itself an organ of society and exists only to contribute a needed result to society, the economy, and the individual. Organs, however, are never defined by what they do, let alone by how they do it. They are defined by their contribution.[32, p.x]

In reading this statement, the bureaucratic administrator might exclaim, "But that's not in my job description!" And indeed it is not. It is a view of the management function that goes far beyond anything conceived of by the bureaucrat.

Drucker presents an exceptionally broad view of the management function. It is one that calls for management to serve as the life-giving organ of the institution it manages, to be capable of turning a mob into a unified body, to relate the institution to the needs of society, and, above all, to make a significant contribution. A large order indeed.

What follows is a set of principles underlying professional management. These principles were drawn from a number of Drucker's works but principally from *Management: Tasks • Responsibillities • Practices.*[32]

As you read these principles, reflect on them. Consider these two questions: (1) Is Drucker's view of professional management sufficient in and of itself to serve as an effective leadership style? (2) What is the relation between professional management and ethics?

1. **The overarching function of management is to achieve organizational objectives through the effective and efficient deployment of human, physical, and financial resources.**

   The individual contributor — say, accountant, engineer, or salesperson — is promoted to the position of management. First and foremost in this person's mind is the question: What is the job of the manager? And further: How does the job of the manager differ from that of the individual contributor?

The move from individual contributor to that of a manager is a quantum leap. As an accountant, engineer, or salesperson, the individual was responsible only for his or her own work. But now, as a manager, the individual is responsible for the work of others. "Getting things done through others" is the classic definition of management.

In addition to being responsible for human resources, the manager is responsible for two other types of resources—physical (facilities, equipment, materials) and financial. The keystone of management is to make sound decisions about the deployment of these three resources—human, physical, and financial—for the purpose of achieving organizational objectives.

2. The manager's job is analogous to that of the orchestra leader.

Gestalt theory tells us that the whole is greater than the sum of its parts. The manager, similar to the conductor of a symphony orchestra, has the job of creating a whole that is greater than the sum of its parts, a productive enterprise that generates more than the sum of the resources put into it.

If the individual musicians played without a common score and without a conductor, what would we have? Just noise. The purpose of the score and the conductor is to meld the individual instruments into pleasing music. And so it is with the manager.

We do not expect the conductor to be capable of playing all of the instruments included in the orchestra. But nevertheless, he or she should be capable of judging the sounds emitted from each instrument—and be able to provide constructive feedback—for the purpose of achieving a common goal.

3. The work of the manager consists of these functions: planning, organizing, staffing and staff development, communicating, motivating, and measuring.

The vast literature on management reveals reasonably good agreement on the basic functions of management:
- **Planning**—creating a road map on how to achieve the organizational objectives.
- **Organizing**—clarifying the roles and responsibilities of each job and linking the various jobs into an efficient structure.

- **Staffing and staff development** — hiring staff and providing the training needed by each person to carry out his or her job.
- **Communicating** — providing the information needed by each employee to carry out the job requirements.
- **Motivating** — providing rewards and incentives that will yield a high level of performance on the part of each employee.
- **Measuring** — evaluating performance in the light of the plans and taking corrective action as appropriate.

4. **Management is an objective function and ought to be grounded in the responsibility for performance — for producing results.**

Indeed, management is an objective function. It is not charisma; it is not some special magic; it is not mysterious. No, it is none of these. Rather, it is an objective function that can be defined, observed, communicated, and measured.

The principal responsibility of management is to produce results. Given the human, physical, and financial resources, the manager is to make efficient and effective use of these resources to produce results. Numerous barriers will be encountered along the way, and problems will abound. But that is what the manager's job is all about — to solve the problems.

The manager is responsible for performance. Not important is the manager's personality. And not important is whether or not the manager is loved by his or her employees. In the final analysis, the manager can be evaluated only on the basis of producing results.

5. **Effective managers set objectives and then go about reaching them in an organized, orderly, and conscious way.**

Perhaps the most powerful tool of management introduced in this century is management by objectives. This approach to management is both a philosophy and a method of management.

As a philosophy, management by objectives means that the manager's job is to set clear objectives and then make sound decisions regarding human, physical, and financial resources to the end of achieving the objectives.

As a method, management by objectives provides a system of managing. Essentially, it involves a process of setting annual objectives, developing a plan to achieve the objectives, establishing an organizational structure that will help achieve the objectives, directing people toward accomplishing the objectives, and measuring performance in the light of the objectives. This is what the process of managing is all about.

6. Managing is a profession just as is accounting or engineering.

When the accountant and the engineer became managers, they joined a new profession. Previously, they had been a member of either the accounting profession or the engineering profession. They were members of their professional associations and subscribed to and read the relevant professional journals. And they practiced either accounting or engineering.

They are now in the profession of management. In this role, they are members of the American Management Association and read such journals as the *Management Review* and the *Harvard Business Review*. But most important, they no longer practice accounting or engineering; they now practice management. This is their new profession.

7. Professional managers view management as a career — their present and future means of livelihood.

Consider the university professor who is to serve as department head for a three-year period in a "rotating chair" assignment. This assignment involves handling the administrative affairs of the department — and perhaps teaching one course per quarter. After the three-year assignment is completed, he or she will return to the full-time job of teaching and research. It is highly unlikely that this professor — during the three-year assignment as department chairperson — considered himself or herself to be a professional manager.

Not so with the manager in business or industry. Here we have an individual who moved from individual contributor to technical leader and then from technical leader to manager. He or she is now on a career path that involves continual advancement up the management ladder.

Most practicing managers would agree that, after a period of three to five years as a manager, there is "a point of no return"— that is, it would not be feasible to return to the position of individual contributor (at least in a highly technical field). A commitment has been made to a career in professional management.

8. **There is a body of management knowledge that can be taught.**

Since the time of the publication of Frederick Taylor's classic book, *Scientific Management,* in 1911, thousands of books on the subject of management have been published. Storing all of these books in a single location would call for an immense library. And storing all of the management journals would require no small amount of space.

Indeed, there is a large body of management knowledge based upon the research of scholars and the experience of practicing managers. Many of the basic texts are organized in a systematic manner (e.g., with chapters on planning, organizing, staffing and staff development, directing and leading, and measuring) — focusing on what effective managers actually do. And importantly, this management knowledge can be taught.

9. **Professional managers are educated, trained, and skilled in management principles, methods, and tools.**

Management education can begin in an undergraduate college program and continue throughout a manager's career. It would be inappropriate for any manager, prior to retirement, to exclaim, "I have arrived." Indeed not, because management education should take place on a continuing basis.

Some excellent management education programs can be found in U. S. colleges and universities. These programs might lead to a bachelor's degree, a master's degree, or even a Ph.D.

With regard to continuing education programs beyond the college and university level, U.S. companies spend billions of dollars on management education programs. Such programs might range from a basic course in "Principles of Management" for new supervisors to one in "Advanced Strategic Planning" for chief executives. Some managers participate in at least one seminar per year throughout their careers.

10. **The professional manager is a lifelong student of the available body of knowledge in the field of management.**

The individual who has made a firm commitment to being a professional manager normally will be reading books and journals different from those he or she was previously reading as an individual contributor. A professional manager is likely to build his or her own professional library, which might include a collection of several of the basic classics in management and several of the current "best sellers." This library helps the manager stay abreast of current principles, methods, and tools of management.

It is evident from these principles that Drucker views management as a profession. He states it clearly when he says:

> Managers practice management. They do not practice economics. They do not practice quantification. They do not practice behavioral science. These are tools for the manager. But he no more practices economics than a physician practices blood testing. He no more practices behavioral sciences than a biologist practices the microscope. He no more practices quantification than a lawyer practices precedents. He practices management.[32, p.17]

Question: Are you convinced? Is management a true profession? Drucker's argument is persuasive. Management is an objective function that is grounded in the responsibility for performance. The job of the manager can be defined in terms of basic functions that are clearly definable. There is a body of knowledge that can be taught. Managers are educated, trained, and skilled in management philosophy, methods, and tools. And large numbers of managers view management as a career — their present and future means of livelihood. True, it is all of these things, but one thing is lacking.

For the field of management to be considered a fully developed profession, it needs a professional association that transcends the individual organization. In a profession, conduct is sanctioned by an association of peers who develop and impose rules, policies, and standards — and serve as a mediary between members of the profession and the public interest. Inasmuch as the field of management lacks such a professional association, we can conclude that management is *almost* a profession just as are medicine, law, and engineering — but not quite.

Because there is no externally sanctioned body that establishes and enforces ethical standards, the governing body becomes the employer — the organization that employs the manager. Each organization has a culture that communicates "how we do things around here." The ground rules for judging appropriate and inappropriate conduct are embedded in the corporate culture.

It is here that we see the close connection between professional management and social contract ethics. The organization establishes

the ground rules for proper conduct. The manager then agrees—
either explicitly or implicitly—to abide by these ground rules in order
to derive the benefits of job security, salary, pension, etc. This mutual
agreement establishes the social contract.

From an ethical standpoint, one of the major problems associated
with pure social contract ethics in organizations is that the collective conscience—or "group think"—may be led astray. Or stated better,
we might say that the collective conscience sometimes leads itself
astray.

Consider the case of the frog. Drop a frog in a tub of hot water,
and it will jump out immediately. But put a frog in a tub of cool
water, and then heat the water gradually until it is boiling. Do you
know what will happen to the frog? Because it automatically ad-
justs to a change in temperature that remains below the threshold
of awareness, it will boil to death. This same phenomenon sometimes
occurs in organizations that are governed by the collective conscience.
Without the person of outspoken opinion who will question and
challenge the collective conscience, the organization may suffer the
same fate as that of the frog.

We can only conclude that, with respect to leadership styles, professional management is a major part of the story—but it is not the
complete story.

THE TRANSFORMING LEADER

In his book, *Leadership,* James MacGregor Burns makes a clear
distinction between two types of leadership—transactional and
transforming. It is instructive to consider the differences between the
two.

According to Burns, the more common type of leadership is
transactional:

> The relations of most leaders and followers are trans-
> actional—leaders approach followers with an eye to ex-
> changing one thing for another: jobs for votes, or subsidies
> for campaign contributions. Such transactions comprise the
> bulk of the relationships among leaders and followers,
> especially in groups, legislatures, and parties.[26, p.4]

Going beyond the political realm, we commonly find numerous
examples of transactional leadership in organizations—which is best

exemplified by the professional management model. Consider, for example, a typical approach to performance appraisal. The supervisor informs his or her staff that their accomplishments with regard to their performance objectives will be documented in a written performance appraisal at the end of the review period. The results of these evaluations will determine, or at least greatly influence, the amount of their annual pay increases. Here we see, either stated or implied, a clear transaction between the supervisor and the employee: "If you perform well, I will reward you monetarily. If you do not perform well, I will not reward you. In essence, I will reward you in proportion to your performance."

There is nothing basically wrong with this approach to performance appraisal and compensation. But if it represents the essential relation between the supervisor and the employee, it is indeed limited with regard to leadership effectiveness. It may achieve a moderate level of performance, but it will not produce outstanding performance. We need more than this simple transactional relation.

The better way is found in transforming leadership. Burns elucidates this second type of leadership:

> *Transforming* leadership, while more complex than transactional leadership, is more potent. The transforming leader recognizes an existing need or demand of a potential follower. But, beyond that, the transforming leader looks for potential motives in followers, seeks to satisfy higher needs, and engages the full person of the follower. . . . Woodrow Wilson called for leaders who, by boldly interpreting the nation's conscience, could lift a people out of their everyday selves. That people can be lifted *into* their better selves is the secret of transforming leadership.[26, p.4, p.462]

This, then, is the principal theme of transforming leadership: *lifting people into their better selves.* Fortunate indeed are those persons who have worked for such leaders.

The principles that follow are intended as a summary of Burns's theory of transforming leadership. They are drawn from his book, *Leadership.*[26] As you read these principles, identify what you believe to be the principal differences between Drucker's professional manager and Burns's transforming leader.

1. Leadership is not merely an attribute or a function, but is a *relationship* between the leader and the followers.

Leadership *as an attribute* focuses on the personality of the leader. Charisma is the personal magic of the leader that arouses the enthusiasm and loyalty of followers. Leadership *as a function* is at the heart of the professional management model. We have identified the overarching function: to manage human, physical, and financial resources for the purpose of achieving organizational objectives.

The importance of charisma and knowledge of the management function is not to be denied. But the essence of transforming leadership is found in the *relationship* between the leader and the followers. "Transforming leadership," notes Burns, "occurs when one or more persons engage with others in such a way that leaders and followers raise one another to higher levels of motivation and morality. Their purposes, which might have started out as separate but related, become fused."[26, p.20]

2. The effective leader takes pleasure in the growth and self-actualization of other people.

Many managers enjoy seeing *themselves* grow, and there is nothing at all wrong with that. A smaller number of managers, however, derive genuine satisfaction from helping *others* grow. Effective leaders take a personal interest in the development of each of their staff. They help remove barriers, they help obtain resources, and they provide effective coaching. Witnessing the growth and development of their people gives them great joy. The feeling that one has contributed to another person's growth is a reward in and of itself.

3. The effective leader views others in terms of their potential.

Many managers view their people only in terms of what they are today or what they have been in the past. Somewhat rare are those managers who view their individual staff members in terms of their potential, in terms of what they might become. But this is what developmental managers do. They perceive both actuality and potentiality. They confirm individuals on the basis of both what they are and what they might become. And they delight in helping to convert potentiality into actuality — in helping their people become what they might become.

4. The effective leader engages the full person of the follower.

I once found myself serving as an outside party in listening to the complaints of a group of secretaries. These secretaries had previously expressed a number of their concerns to the division director and other managers, and I was requested by the division director to meet with the secretaries, to "hear them out," and then to pass on their concerns to management. I recall from this meeting one complaint in particular. Mary spoke with considerable emotion as she described the uncaring attitude of her immediate supervisor. And what "bugged" her the most was that he referred to her as "Bionic Fingers."

Many are those managers who view their people only in terms of the functions they perform. Not so with the transforming leader. This leader views each employee as a total human being, as a person of worth. In keeping with the philosophy of Immanuel Kant, each person is viewed as an end in himself or herself, not merely as a means to some other end.

5. The effective leader is able to identify values and motives of followers and appeal to these values and motives.

By taking a personal interest in the development of each of his or her people, the transforming leader gets to know them as individual persons. This knowledge includes how they see themselves today and how they would like to see themselves in the future. It includes knowledge of their values — their basic ground rules for making decisions. And it includes knowledge of their principal motivators — what spurs them to act.

This knowledge is essential if the leader-follower relationship is to be effective. And it should be noted that the knowledge about the individual person is obtained and used in an honest and open manner. The approach here would be considered the polar opposite of that used by the manipulators in trying to figure out "what button to push."

6. The effective leader is able to elevate the values and motives of followers.

The transforming leader does not stop with the knowledge of the follower's *present* values and motives. This is merely the starting point. Beyond that, the leadership strategy involves elevating these values and motives to ever higher levels. Recall Abraham Maslow's five-tiered hierarchy of human needs — physiological to safety to belongingness to self-esteem to self-actualization. What the transforming leader is doing is facilitating the movement of each person up the hierarchy, and as a consequence of each advancement, *new values and motives emerge.*

7. The effective leader motivates others through empowerment.

Transactional leadership relies on the carrot-and-stick approach to motivation. The "carrot" is held out by the supervisor in the form of possible rewards — pay increase, promotion, better job assignment, etc. If these potential rewards do not work, then lurking in the background is the "stick" in the form of possible punishments — no pay increase, no promotion, a worse job assignment, etc. This is the pure market economy. We are talking about commodities in exchange for labor. There is nothing really complex about the underlying rationale, and it is accepted by no small number of managers as iron-clad logic.

Burns proposes an alternative to the carrot-and-stick approach to motivation. As its principal means of motivation, transforming leadership relies on empowerment. With power being defined as the capability for doing or accomplishing something, empowerment means to give power to followers. Leaders empower their people by increasing their capability for doing or accomplishing something. When leaders empower their people, a remarkable thing happens: the leaders themselves *gain in power.* As one side of the coin is enlarged, the other side also increases.

8. The effective leader is a good coach.

Some managers view coaching of staff as a luxury. If all their "primary" duties are taken care of, and they have time to spare, then they might devote some time to coaching. Staff development simply is not perceived as a core function.

Not so with transforming leaders. These leaders place coaching right in the core of their job functions. They consider coaching to be just as important as any of their other job functions, and they are willing to be held accountable for how well they develop their people. In fact, they evaluate their own performance on the basis of how much their people are learning, growing, and expanding in job responsibilities.

9. The effective leader helps others become leaders.

Perhaps the leader's greatest challenge is to help followers become leaders. This is one of the principal goals that distinguishes the transforming leader from the Lone Ranger. The masked rider has only Tonto, who is expected to remain a follower. But the transforming leader views his or her followers as potential leaders. By serving as a role model, by providing appropriate job opportunities, and by coaching, the potentiality is transformed into actuality. The essential requirement, of course, is commitment on the part of the leader.

10. Leaders are judged in the balance sheet of history by their impact on the well-being of the persons whose lives they touched.

It is interesting to speculate on how long the four different types of leaders will be remembered. The manipulator may be remembered only until one "gets even," and if longer, it will be a negative memory. The bureaucratic administrator will be quickly forgotten, because he or she will be viewed more as a functionary than as a person. The professional manager may be remembered a reasonably long time if he or she had a significant impact on the organization. But the one who will be remembered the longest undoubtedly will be the transforming leader. This is the leader who lifted others up, lifted them to their better selves. And the followers realize that they would not be the persons they now are if it had not been for their leader. And miracle of miracles: the followers are now becoming transforming leaders who are actively engaged in lifting others to their better selves — and we witness a true multiplier effect.

What is presented in these few pages is a description of effective leadership. The essence of leadership is not found in manipulating others to further one's own ends, and it is not found in communicating and enforcing rules. Nor is it found exclusively in managing human, physical, and financial resources for the purpose of achieving organizational objectives. Rather, the essence of leadership is found in *leading people*. It is found in the relationship between leader and follower that helps lift both to their better selves. This is what leadership is all about. The manager who has grasped this basic truth about leadership has advanced a giant step in his or her own development.

For the manager who has advanced to this stage of development *in actual practice*, there will be a number of substantial benefits. First, as a result of the authentic environment created by transforming leadership, there will be no place for cunning, deception, and subterfuge. Second, as a consequence of the high degree of responsibility of the individual staff members, there will be no need for a large number of rules. And third, as a result of the high degree of self-management witnessed in the staff members, there will be no need for the manager to spend a great amount of time in directing and controlling the work of others. These are no small benefits! What it all boils down to is that *the leader will have more time to lead.*

This is what Burns's theory of transforming leadership is all about. Its implications for the field of management are profound. Burns, perhaps better than any other, perceived the close relation between leadership style and ethics. He offers this key observation:

> *Transforming* leadership occurs when one or more persons *engage* with others in such a way that leaders and followers raise one another to higher levels of motivation and morality. . . . Such leadership ultimately becomes *moral* in that it raises the level of human conduct and aspiration of both leader and led, and thus it has a transforming effect on both.[26, p.20]

Consider carefully what Burns is saying. There is great wisdom in this passage.

Burns's first point is that leaders and followers can raise one another to higher levels of motivation and morality. Certainly, we would expect the leader to lift the followers to higher levels of motivation and morality, but can we expect the followers to do likewise with the leader? Indeed, it does happen. Consider, for example, a unit manager who has made a special effort to promote ethical conduct among all members of the unit. And suppose that this has been achieved as actual fact. Then, on a given day and under considerable pressure to make a "good" decision, the manager is found vacillating on an ethical issue. (Remember: ethical conduct is a variable, not a constant.) What may very well happen is that *the staff will nudge the manager toward the ethical response* — that is, to the "right-good" decision. It is as though the relationship between the leader and the followers has become symbiotic: the followers need the leader, but the leader also needs the followers.

Burns's second point is that lifting others to their better selves ultimately becomes *moral*. This observation can best be understood by considering it in the light of Maslow's hierarchy of human needs. Essentially, what the transforming leader is doing is to help lift others up the hierarchy. What happens when an individual moves up the hierarchy is that higher level values, which were previously unconscious, now become conscious. At the bottom of the hierarchy, the individual's consciousness was limited to such lower level values as survival, safety, protection, etc. But now moving toward the top of the hierarchy, the individual becomes conscious of such higher level values as truth, goodness, equality, justice, etc. Most would agree that the second set of values constitutes a higher level of morality than the first.

Given this summary of transforming leadership, we will end with a challenge from Burns to each and every leader:

> The great bulk of leadership activity consists of the day-to-day interaction of leaders and followers. But the ultimate test of moral leadership is its capacity to transcend the claims of the multiplicity of everyday wants and needs and expectations, to respond to the higher levels of moral development, and to relate leadership behavior — its roles, choices, style, commitments — to a set of reasoned, relatively explicit, conscious values.[26, p.46]

SUMMING UP

Given this summary of four different leadership styles and the corresponding ethical systems, we can now outline an Encompassing theory of leadership. This outline will integrate what has been said thus far and highlight its implications.

To begin, picture in your mind's eye a three-sided pyramid. In addition to being only three-sided, the pyramid has two other distinguishing features: the stones are arranged on each side of the pyramid in four tiers, and there is a large concrete rod embedded vertically — from top to bottom — in the center of the pyramid. The three sides represent, respectively, levels of being, ethical systems, and leadership styles. The four tiers represent, respectively from side to side, the four levels of being, the four ethical systems, and the four leadership styles. And the concrete rod that penetrates all four tiers and holds the pyramid intact represents reason. We will consider each in turn.

Circling the pyramid, we note the alignment of the tiers — as shown in Figure 21. At the first tier, we see empirical existence, end-result ethics, and manipulative leadership. At the second tier, we see consciousness at large, rule ethics, and bureaucratic administration. At the third tier, we see spirit, social contract ethics, and professional management. Then at the top tier, we see Existenz, personalistic ethics, and transforming leadership. It fits together nicely. The key point to appreciate here is that, generally speaking, one's level of being leads to a particular ethical system, and one's ethical system leads to a particular leadership style.

Now we focus on one side of the pyramid, which we will call the "first" side. Glancing from the bottom to the top, we see the four levels of being — empirical existence, consciousness at large, spirit, and Existenz. It is important to recall that the lower levels do not include the higher levels, but the higher levels include — and give direction to — the lower levels.

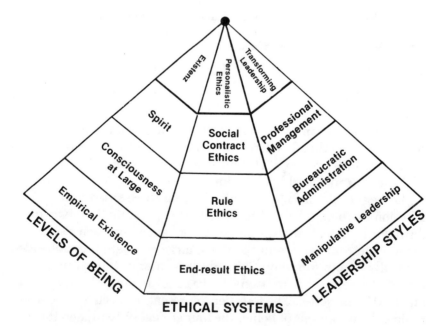

Figure 21.   The "open" pyramid showing the alignment of levels of
being, ethical systems, and leadership styles.

It also is important to recall that the four levels of being are linked together through reason (the concrete rod). The central tenet about this side of the pyramid is that the person of integrity lives out of the Encompassing, which means that this person has risen to the fourth tier of the pyramid, but is at home in the other three tiers, and is guided by reason.

We then look at the second side of the pyramid. Glancing from the bottom to the top, we see the four ethical systems: end-result ethics, rule ethics, social contract ethics, and personalistic ethics. We recall that each ethical system has a different locus of authority: end-result ethics — expected consequences; rule ethics — laws and standards; social contract ethics — the customs and norms of the community; and personalistic ethics — one's conscience. Consistent with the first side of the pyramid, our principal tenet here is that the person who lives out of the Encompassing will have achieved the level of personalistic ethics, but will see a place for the other three ethical systems, and will be guided by reason.

We now move to the third side of the pyramid. Again, glancing from the bottom to the top, we see four leadership styles: manipulative leadership, bureaucratic administration, professional management, and transforming leadership.

We recall that each leadership style projects a different view of its principal function: manipulative leadership - to use cunning and deception to further one's own ends; bureaucratic administration — to communicate and enforce rules; professional management — to make decisions about human, physical, and financial resources for the purpose of achieving organizational objectives; and transforming leadership — to lift followers to their better selves.

To get things done, each of these four types of leaders uses power. But the sources of power are radically different: manipulative leadership — coalitions formed through chicanery; bureaucratic administration — position in the organization; professional management — knowledge and experience in the principles and methods of management; and transforming leadership — the empowerment of followers.

Given these four leadership styles, the question then becomes: Suppose that a manager has made a commitment to living out of the Encompassing — and achieving true integrity — what is the corresponding leadership style? There is an all-too-obvious answer — *an Encompassing approach to leadership.*

The principal message of Encompassing leadership is that we can find a place for all four leadership styles. Under the guidance of reason, each can contribute to our coping with ethical issues and making right-good decisions.

Each leadership style can make a significant contribution (but is insufficient when used alone):

- We accept from manipulative leadership the importance of power to leadership effectiveness, but reject the cunning and deception.
- We accept from bureaucratic administration the importance of rules and regulations, but become distraught when these rules and regulations become ends in themselves.
- We accept from professional management the importance of producing results, but become concerned when human resources are viewed merely as another resource alongside physical resources and financial resources that must be managed for the purpose of achieving organizational objectives.
- We become inspired by transforming leadership and its emphasis on the empowerment of followers, but realize that this is not the total job of management.

By analyzing the strengths and limitations of each of these four leadership styles — through the active use of our reason — we realize that there is a place for each in our Encompassing approach to leadership. While no one of them is up to the total task, each can make a significant contribution to the whole.

We now ask: What is the appropriate label for the manager who applies an Encompassing approach to leadership? We can keep it simple: *the effective leader-manager.*

Within the framework provided by the Encompassing and the four leadership styles, we can say that the effective leader-manager has these attributes: (1) possesses the tools of power and knows how to use them; (2) establishes boundary conditions for the purpose of achieving greater effectiveness and efficiency; (3) formulates clear purpose and effectively manages resources to achieve the purpose; (4) lifts followers to their better selves through empowerment; and (5) is guided throughout by the use of reason.

Most important is that the effective leader-manager is a person of integrity. This is the spark that casts the light. And, through the generation of trust, this is the spark that contributes to long-term success.

If you accept the Encompassing theory of leadership, then you should be aware of several important implications. These concern manager selection, manager assignment, manager development, and the need for positive reinforcement. We will consider each in turn.

1. **When selecting a person for a management position, give considerable attention to the person's ethical values.**

    As an idealist, I would like to think that organizations would endeavor to select managers who had achieved the level of personalistic ethics — the top tier of the pyramid. But, as a pragmatist, I know that managers who have achieved that level of ethical maturity are not in plentiful supply. Also, I can appreciate the practicality of getting a match between the ethical values of the new manager and those of the organization. To this end, it is important that an organization give careful consideration to the type of manager it wants — with respect to the person's ethical values — and then go after that kind of person.

    A carefully planned in-depth interview can assist in identifying the ethical values of a prospective manager. An effective interview strategy is to present the candidate with a variety of "cases" involving both an economic concern and an ethical concern. (These cases might be drawn from either the organization's own experience or the cases presented in Chapter II.) Then judge each response on the basis of these four categories: neither good nor right, good but not right, right but not good, both good and right. Also, probe to identify what appears to be the candidate's primary locus of authority: expected consequences, laws and rules, customs and norms of the community, or conscience. Through this process, a trained interviewer should be able to make an accurate assessment of each candidate's ethical values.

2. **When assigning a manager to a particular organizational unit, take into consideration the relation between the manager's ethical values and those of the unit members.**

    Consider the case in which an organization that is known for being reasonably ethical assigns a new manager who operates at the level of end-result ethics to head up a department in which the members have been operating at the level of rule ethics. A considerable amount of conflict can be expected, because the new manager will focus on achieving results (regardless of the means employed), whereas the department staff will feel compelled to follow policies, procedures, and rules.

Consider a second case in which an organization assigns a new manager who operates at the level of rule ethics to a department in which the members have been operating at the level of personalistic ethics. Again, a considerable amount of conflict can be expected, because the manager will be focusing on systems, procedures, and rules, whereas the department staff will be calling for freedom and individual responsibility.

These scenarios should serve to remind us of a basic tenet of Burns's theory of transforming leadership: *for a leader to be able to lift followers to their better selves, the leader must be at a higher level of being than that of the followers.*

3. **When developing an ethics course for managers, involve top management.**

A number of organizations are now developing their own ethics programs for their managers. And this is commendable. But there are two radically different ways of undertaking this activity, one bad and one good.

The approach that should *not* be taken is for upper management to delegate the entire developmental activity to the training department, with the instructions—"Put together an ethics course for our managers as soon as possible." The outcome of this undertaking undoubtedly will turn out far less than desirable. (This is not intended as a lack of faith in training departments, but as a criticism of upper management for abdicating its responsibility.)

Far more effective would be to actively involve upper management—including the chief executive—in the design process. A task force charged with designing the course would consist of several members of upper management and one or more instructional specialists from the training department. Working as a team, this group would answer three basic questions: (1) Where are we now? (2) Where do we want to go? and (3) How do we plan to get there? Early in the developmental process, the team would need to decide which particular ethical system would be promoted. And equally important, the group would have to decide how best to build into the program the organization's tradition, its culture, and its principal values. Thus, it should be clear why this developmental activity cannot simply be delegated to the training department.

4. When evaluating employees on their ethical conduct, apply positive reinforcement.

After visiting with a number of managers to discuss their ethics programs—and reflecting on these visits—I have several concerns. One concern in particular is the negative approach to ethical conduct that is found in no small number of organizations. Many of these programs can best be described as punitive. This is evidenced by ethical codes written only to protect the company, the "hot line" function for reporting offenders, rules for the protection of whistle blowers, written policies and procedures that spell out disciplinary action, etc. Certainly, these measures cannot be dismissed out of hand, but when they constitute the *core* of an ethics program, one begins to wonder about the overall intent of the program.

I have asked several upper-level managers why their approach to ethics focuses more on punishing "wrong" behavior than on reinforcing "right" behavior. This is a typical response: "We expect ethical conduct on the part of *all* of our people. This is a given; it is not something that is negotiable. Hence, we must punish the transgressors."

This attitude has sometimes been referred to as the "slipping through the net" view: "Practically all of the people in our organization are ethical. But occasionally a few rascals will slip through the screening process. Our job is to weed out the rascals."

The implicit assumption underlying this attitude is that ethics is a binary concept, meaning that there are two types of people— the ethical and the unethical. Such simplistic thinking ignores the real-world observation that ethical conduct falls on a continuum, and that practically every human being moves up and down on this continuum. (Some only slightly, and some a great deal.) Ethical conduct is a variable, not a constant.

Given this view of ethical conduct, the challenge at this hour is for leader-managers to take a *positive approach* in dealing with ethical conduct. We know from years of research and experience that we pretty much get the behavior that we reward. So reward ethical conduct! We also know from years of research and experience that, as a means of altering behavior, positive reinforcement is more effective than negative reinforcement. So provide positive reinforcement for ethical conduct! As the saying goes: "Catch people doing things *right.*" What we are calling for, with regard to a positive approach to ethical conduct, is a "paradigm shift."

These are just a few of the implications that fall out of the Encompassing theory of leadership. I am sure that you can think of others. The main point to appreciate is that the theory does indeed provide guidance for practice. The theme throughout is "translating theory into practice." It was Kurt Lewin, the social psychologist, who never tired of saying, "There is nothing so practical as a good theory."

VI

What Should Be Done

Excellent companies do more than talk ethics. They take
positive steps to address ethical issues and apply the practical tools of ethics in their management practice. The application of ethics does not require that managers abdicate
their responsibilities or turn the company into a debating
society. Instead, integrating ethics and management practice helps managers to work more effectively and improve
overall performance in their organizations.

Mark Pastin
"Ethics and Excellence"[99]

---

*A Strategy for Ethical Decision Making • Stating the Mission • Clarifying
the Values • Formulating a Code of Ethics • Developing an Ethics Program • Summing Up*

A STRATEGY FOR ETHICAL DECISION MAKING

Given the theoretical considerations about ethics, leadership, and the
relation between ethics and leadership, we now turn to what perhaps
is the most important question: What should be done? How do we
translate the theory into practice?

With regard to ethical conduct, the leader-manager has a twofold
responsibility: to make ethical decisions and to create a climate that
fosters ethical conduct on the part of his or her staff. To this end,
the leader-manager must do two things: (1) develop a strategy for
making ethical decisions and (2) develop and implement a plan of

action for promoting ethical conduct. We will consider each of these two needs.

The first section of the chapter deals with developing a strategy for ethical decision making. The following four sections deal with developing a plan of action for promoting ethical conduct.

The importance of strategy in decision making has been pointed up by Robert Gilbreath:

> Most successful corporations have discovered that decision making is most effective when supported by a strategy. Each choice is tested by asking: Does it contribute to the overriding strategy? . . . An ethical framework is no more than a personal strategy in this regard. Countless questions about a decision's immediate and ultimate consequences can be avoided by testing each alternative this way: Does it fit my ethical framework?[45]

Innumerable books and papers have been published on the subject of managerial decision making. The various decision making strategies presented in these books and papers deal primarily with the economic dimension of decision making — focusing on such objective criteria as revenue, profit, return on investment, and cash flow.

A decision making strategy that typifies the economic school would go something like this:

1. State the objective to be achieved or the problem to be solved.
2. Establish level of aspiration.
3. Develop alternative solutions.
4. Identify the probable consequences of each alternative.
5. Rank the probable consequences in order of their desirability.
6. Select what appears to be the best alternative in view of the probable consequences.
7. Implement the chosen alternative.

Now there is nothing basically wrong with this decision making strategy. It is logical, objective, and systematic, and it has proved its usefulness. But if it does not accommodate the ethical dimension of decision making, then it is indeed limited. If it cannot take into consideration such criteria as compassion, fairness, honesty, and responsibility, then it can be considered only a limited decision making model.

To include the ethical dimension in our decision making process, it is worthwhile to once again list the four requirements for ethical decision making articulated by James Rest:

1. The person must be able to make some sort of *interpretation* of the particular situation in terms of what actions are possible.
2. The person must be able to make a *judgment* about which course of action is ethically right.
3. The person must *give priority* to ethical values above other personal values such that a decision is made to intend to do what is ethically right.
4. The person must have sufficient perseverance, ego strength, and implementation skills to be able to *follow through* on his or her intention.[103, p.3]

This list of requirements gets at the very heart of ethical decision making. It clearly defines a four-step decision making process: (1) identify alternative courses of action; (2) determine which courses of action are ethically right; (3) give priority to ethical values over egoistic values; and (4) persevere in implementing your preferred alternative.

Another strategy for ethical decision making has been formulated by Laura Nash in the form of a list of questions for examining the ethics of a business decision. The questions, presented in Figure 22, are well targeted and warrant careful study. Giving consideration to these questions whenever making a decision that involves an ethical issue should, in all probability, lead to a "right" decision.

Here there might be some confusion. On the one hand, we have presented a decision making strategy that focuses primarily on the economic dimension. On the other hand, we have presented two strategies that focus primarily on the ethical dimension. Inasmuch as many decisions involve both dimensions, trying to apply two or more different strategies would only confound the situation. There obviously is a need for a single decision making strategy that can deal with both the economic dimension and the ethical dimension.

Recall the two-dimensional framework in Chapter II that defined right-good decisions. The economic dimension encompasses good and bad decisions, whereas the ethical dimension encompasses right and wrong decisions. A sound decision making strategy will lead to right-good decisions, meaning that the decisions are good from an economic standpoint and right from an ethical standpoint. This concept is the point of departure for our proposed decision making strategy.

The watershed postulate of the proposed strategy is that the person of true integrity lives out of the Encompassing. Having advanced

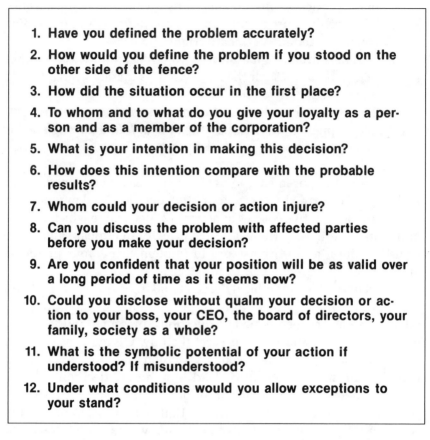

1. Have you defined the problem accurately?

2. How would you define the problem if you stood on the other side of the fence?

3. How did the situation occur in the first place?

4. To whom and to what do you give your loyalty as a person and as a member of the corporation?

5. What is your intention in making this decision?

6. How does this intention compare with the probable results?

7. Whom could your decision or action injure?

8. Can you discuss the problem with affected parties before you make your decision?

9. Are you confident that your position will be as valid over a long period of time as it seems now?

10. Could you disclose without qualm your decision or action to your boss, your CEO, the board of directors, your family, society as a whole?

11. What is the symbolic potential of your action if understood? If misunderstood?

12. Under what conditions would you allow exceptions to your stand?

Laura Nash: "Ethics Without the Sermon"

Figure 22. Twelve questions for examining the ethics of a business decision.

to this level in his or her moral development, the effective leader-manager is guided by an Encompassing theory of ethics.

An Encompassing theory of ethics has a vital role for each of the four ethical systems. Each can facilitate the decision making process and assist in making right-good decisions. As shown in Figure 23, there are four particular tests aligned with the four ethical systems. End-result ethics points up the need to test for expected results. Rule ethics stresses the need to test for policies and procedures. Social contract ethics emphasizes the need to test for organizational values. And

ETHICAL SYSTEMS	DECISION MAKING STRATEGY
End-result Ethics	Test for results
Rule Ethics	Test for policies and procedures
Social Contract Ethics	Test for organizational values
Personalistic Ethics	Test for personal conviction

Figure 23.   Relation between ethical systems and decision making strategy.

finally, personalistic ethics points up the need to test for personal conviction. Involved in all of these tests, of course, is the active use of reason.

The Encompassing decision making strategy is shown in Figure 24. We begin the process with an ethical issue that involves choosing between or among two or more alternatives and ending with one of these alternatives that would be judged to be a right-good decision. In between, we conduct a series of tests — moving from the observable and objective to the experiential and subjective. The entire series of tests is guided by reason.

To illustrate the application of the strategy, we will consider a real-world managerial decision that involves an ethical dilemma. Assume that you are a department manager who has just been notified that you are to be promoted to the level of director and that you are to select your replacement. You have three section managers as your direct reports, and you plan to select one of them as your replacement.

These are the three section managers:

Herbert is your most senior section manager. He is 60 years

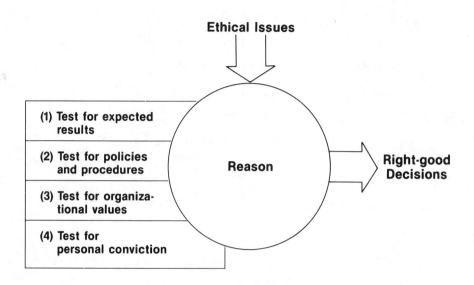

Figure 24.   An Encompassing decision making strategy.

old, has been with the organization for 30 years, and has been a section manager for 12 years. As a conscientious and reliable employee, Herbert has filled in for you a number of times over the years and has done a creditable job. A major reason why Herbert would like your job is that the promotion would lead to an automatic pay increase, and his pension will be based upon the average salary of the top five years. While he would be no dynamo, Herbert could take over your job immediately.

Florence is the second in age and seniority. She is 42 years old, has been with the organization for 12 years, and has been a section manager for three years. Florence is intelligent, has an excellent grasp of her job, and has superb people skills. She is a very competent manager and desires to move up the management ladder. Inasmuch as she has never filled in for you in your absence, it would take her about three months to feel comfortable in your job.

Richard is the third in age and seniority. He is 28 years old, has been with the organization for six years, and has been a section manager for just under one year. With regard to technical competence, Richard is the best in the entire department. He is extremely intelligent, learns quickly, and has an excellent grasp of the most complex operations of the department. Richard is viewed as a technical expert by the staff and is in high demand as a consultant on difficult technical problems. If he were to be made a department manager, he would be a technical leader of the highest order. But inasmuch as he has had limited management experience, it would take him at least 12 months to learn your job.

These, then, are the three candidates for your position. Which one would you select?

The Encompassing decision making strategy would go something like this:

You have a clear objective: to select a competent manager who can replace you immediately. And you have three candidates: Herbert, Florence, and Richard.

Beginning the decision making process with end-result ethics, we would focus on expected consequences. All three of the candidates could be expected to do a reasonably good job as department manager. In terms of the time frame for learning the job, Herbert could take over immediately, Florence would take somewhat longer, and Richard would take even longer. Herbert would be competent but certainly not outstanding. Florence would be a solid performer. In the long run, Richard might be an outstanding performer and might very well move on to become a vice president. Not enough here to provide the answer, so we move on.

Reflecting next on rule ethics, we consider the organization's relevant policies and procedures. With regard to promotions, the organization has a clear policy that requires promotion from within, assuming that there are qualified candidates. The policy also states that the promotion decision should be based upon past performance and future potential. This last requirement may eliminate Herbert, but we are still okay with Florence and Richard.

Moving next to social contract ethics, we consider the organization's values. One value in particular that is most relevant to this situation is equal opportunity. As an equal opportunity employer, the organization has made a strong commitment to affirmative action. And now, with Florence, we have a candidate who has a proven track record and the potential for being an excellent department manager. At this stage in the process, we probably would lean toward Florence.

Now at the last step in the series of tests, we are guided by personalistic ethics and our personal convictions. And once again, Herbert emerges as a live candidate — because of his long tenure with the organization and his dedicated service and loyalty. Also, as humanistic managers, we would not ignore Herbert's desire to have a larger pension at the time of retirement.

So much for the tests at the four stages in the process. We now must pull back from scrutinizing the individual trees and gaze at the forest. In other words, taking into consideration the ideas gleaned from the detailed analysis, we must now consider the total situation. This includes the time frame: both the short-term consequences and the long-term consequences. And it includes consideration of all stakeholders: what is best for the organization, for the candidates, and for you as the director who will be responsible for the new department manager. Penetrating all of these considerations is the active use of reason.

Given this analysis, it is now time to make the decision. Which of the three candidates would you select?

What we have illustrated here is an example of ethical reasoning. And it is ethical reasoning carried out in the light of the Encompassing.

This Encompassing decision making strategy is both generic and specific. It is sufficiently generic to be applicable to practically any ethical issue with which a manager might be confronted. Yet it is sufficiently specific to serve as a step-by-step decision making process. The challenge for each manager is to adapt the process to his or her particular situation.

Our underlying thesis is that every manager needs a strategy such as the above for making ethical decisions. Without such a strategy, the manager is likely to end up in a quagmire of confusion, indecisiveness, rationalizations, and guilt.

To be able to implement the proposed Encompassing decision making strategy, several organizational requirements are called for. These are the ones that I believe are most salient:

1. To test for expected results, managers need a clear statement of purpose.
2. To test for policies and procedures, managers need a written code of ethics.
3. To test for organizational values, managers need a written statement of these values.
4. To test for personal conviction, managers need to understand their own values and system of ethics.

5. To be able to fully employ the Encompassing decision making strategy, managers need to understand ethics and have the ability to engage in ethical reasoning.

It is to these organizational requirements that the next four sections are addressed. Collectively and sequentially, the four sections are intended to serve as a plan of action for promoting ethical conduct. Please note that some version of this plan of action, as outlined in Figure 25, could be implemented by every manager in the organization, regardless of level or function.

STATING THE MISSION

In the course of conducting on-site management seminars for managers from the same organization, I continue to be surprised at the number of managers who do not have a clear understanding of their organization's mission. I frequently ask the participating managers this question: What is your organization's mission? What is its reason for existence? The answers will be varied. One manager responds, "Our purpose is to make money." Then another responds, "No, that's not our primary mission. Our actual mission is to provide a quality product for our customers." Then still a third responds, "No, I disagree with both of the previous statements. I think that our primary mission is to survive."

STEP 1: State the mission

STEP 2: Clarify the values

STEP 3: Formulate a code of ethics

STEP 4: Develop an ethics program

Figure 25. A plan of action for promoting ethical conduct.

And so it goes. After hearing several different mission statements — and each expressed with conviction — the seminar participants then look at each other somewhat befuddled. They realize that they do not actually know the mission of their organization.

In his book, *Eupsychian Management,* Abraham Maslow points up the importance of having a clear sense of purpose:

> It seems very clear to me that in an enterprise, if everybody concerned is absolutely clear about the goals and directives and far purposes of the organization, practically all other questions then become simple technical questions of fitting means to the ends. But it is also true that to the extent that these far goals are confused or conflicting or ambivalent or only partially understood, then all the discussion of techniques and methods and means is of little use.[80, p.41]

Perhaps the point is somewhat overstated, but only slightly. It is true that, if every member of an organization has a clear understanding of the organization's mission, then other things seem to fall in place. Without this understanding, there is lack of direction, uncertainty, and confusion.

One problem associated with organizational mission is that we sometimes find that upper management has not given deep thought to the matter. If managers at this level are not clear on the overall purpose of the organization, how can they expect the first-level and middle-level managers to understand what the organization is all about?

"I have never really thought about the overall purpose of my firm." This was the statement made by the president of a small engineering firm to the other members of one of my management seminars. After receiving much encouragement from the class members, the young president began to work during the evening hours on his company's mission statement. Over a three-day period, he proceeded to "try out" several versions of the mission statement on the class. It was not until the final day of the seminar that he presented one that was generally accepted by the class. To the round of applause received, the president bowed in appreciation. This was indeed a significant accomplishment.

A second problem associated with some mission statements is that they do not consider all stakeholders. For example: What should be the mission statement for a restaurant chain? The president of such a chain once presented me a "first draft" of a management philosophy for my review. The written management philosophy, which was to be distributed to all employees, included this statement of mission: "To maximize the financial return for the owners." I was able to convince the president that this was not the most appropriate statement of mission. He later formulated what appeared to be a more appropriate mission statement: "To provide quality food and service at a reasonable price." This revised version of an overall purpose is one to which all stakeholders should be able to relate. And if it is achieved, then the profits should be forthcoming. As Peter Drucker has aptly said, profit is not the organization's mission, but the *reward* that the organization receives for achieving the mission.

Still a third problem is that the members of a given organization (or organizational unit) may have different perceptions or understandings of the mission. This problem was brought home to me some years ago during the course of conducting a management seminar for 20 members of an auditing department. Each of the participants was asked to write the department's mission and then present it to the class. About half of the participants wrote a mission statement that focused on "regulating and controlling," whereas the other half wrote one that focused on "assisting and facilitating." Different indeed are these two views of the department's mission, and which one is selected will have a profound impact on the attitudes and actions of the department's staff.

These are common problems associated with organizational missions. The important thing is for every leader-manager to be aware of these problems and do whatever possible to obviate them.

Our thesis here is that every manager should take the responsibility for formulating a clear statement of mission for the organization or organizational unit for which he or she is responsible.

An acceptable mission statement will have these attributes:
1. It will clearly define the purpose of the organization (or organizational unit) — its reason for existence.
2. It will focus on the product or service to be provided and will be sufficiently comprehensive to include all products or services.
3. It will be sufficiently focused to point up uniqueness.
4. It will be responsive to the needs and expectations of various stakeholders.
5. It will be energizing to all members of the organization.
6. It will provide direction for decision making and action.
7. It will be enduring (but not set in concrete).

Regarding the last point, it is important to appreciate that, over time, missions do change. Battelle, for example, has witnessed a significant change in mission. As one of the world's largest independent research organizations, Battelle for some years stressed the theme of "advancing science for the benefit of humankind." Today, the mission is "putting technology to work." This change in mission is having a significant impact on all of the management functions: planning, organizing, staffing and staff development, communicating, motivating, and measuring.

Writing a mission statement that satisfies all seven of the above criteria is no simple matter. It requires a deep understanding of what the organization now is as well as what it might become. And it requires a deep understanding of the needs and expectations of the various stakeholders. In essence, it requires deep thought.

This deep thought should lead to the following actions on the part of every manager:

1. Define a "crystal-clear" mission for the organization (or organizational unit).
2. Communicate the mission to all stakeholders.
3. Make decisions and take actions in the light of the mission.
4. Evaluate performance in the light of the mission.

Following this strategy will help translate the mission statement into practice. The mission will become a reality: it will direct the course of daily actions.

Making the mission a reality will yield a number of benefits. Included here will be a compass that provides direction, better staff motivation and morale, and greater confidence in management on the part of the staff. And most important: the mission statement can serve as a beacon that aids in making right-good decisions.

CLARIFYING THE VALUES

In their book *Corporate Cultures*, Deal and Kennedy stress that successful companies place a strong emphasis on values. They found that these companies share three characteristics:

- They stand for something — that is, they have a clear and explicit philosophy about how they aim to conduct their business.
- Management pays a great deal of attention to shaping and fine-tuning these values to conform to the economic and busi-

ness environment of the company and to communicating them to the organization.

- These values are known and shared by all the people who work for the company—from the production worker right through the ranks of senior management.[30, p.22]

Our basic thesis here is that every organization should have a written statement of values. These values should communicate what the organization stands for—its basic ground rules. Further, it should be a principal responsibility of every manager to translate the organizational values into practice.

An acceptable statement of values would have these attributes:

1. The values are clearly defined.
2. They represent the principal ground rules that guide daily conduct.
3. They respond to all stakeholders (customers, employees, the general community, and stockholders).
4. They are reasonably consistent with reality.
5. They are internally consistent.
6. They provide guidance for decision making and action.

Johnson & Johnson, a company that has received a great deal of press since the time of the Tylenol recall, has a clear set of values in the form of a credo. As a company that receives very high marks on ethics, Johnson & Johnson actively promotes its basic values throughout the organization. The company's credo is shown in Figure 26, and an extraction of the basic values is presented in Figure 27. This credo and the values could serve as an excellent paradigm for many organizations.

Once the basic values are elucidated, the question then becomes: What should be done to make certain that organizational values are put into practice? More specifically, what should each manager do to assure that the values are translated into a reality that is manifest in the staff's daily behavior?

It is generally agreed that the manager serves as the focal point for the organization's value system. Staff members look to the manager for cues to determine what constitutes acceptable and unacceptable behavior within the organization. The daily decisions and actions of the manager reflect more than anything else the organization's *actual values*. Therefore, it is incumbent on every manager to understand fully the organization's values, to internalize these values,

JOHNSON & JOHNSON CREDO

We believe our first responsibility is to the doctors,
nurses, and patients, to mothers and all others who
use our products and services. In meeting their needs,
everything we do must be of high quality. We must constantly strive to reduce our costs in order to maintain
reasonable prices. Customers' orders must be serviced
promptly and accurately. Our suppliers and distributors
must have an opportunity to make a fair profit.

We are responsible to our employees, the men and
women who work with us throughout the world. Everyone must be considered as an individual. We must
respect their dignity and recognize their merit. Compensation must be fair and adequate, and working conditions clean, orderly, and safe. Employees must feel free
to make suggestions and complaints. There must be
equal opportunity for employment, development, and
advancement for those qualified. We must provide competent management, and their actions must be just and
ethical.

We are responsible to the communities in which we
live and work and to the world community as well. We
must be good citizens—support good works and charities and bear our fair share of taxes. We must encourage civic improvements and better health and
education. We must maintain in good order the property we are privileged to use, protecting the environment and natural resources.

Our final responsibility is to our stockholders. Business
must make a sound profit. We must experiment with
new ideas. Research must be carried on, innovative programs developed, and mistakes paid for. New equipment must be purchased, new facilities provided, and
new products launched. Reserves must be created to
provide for adverse times. When we operate according
to these principles, the stockholders should realize a
fair return.

Figure 26.   Illustrative organizational values.

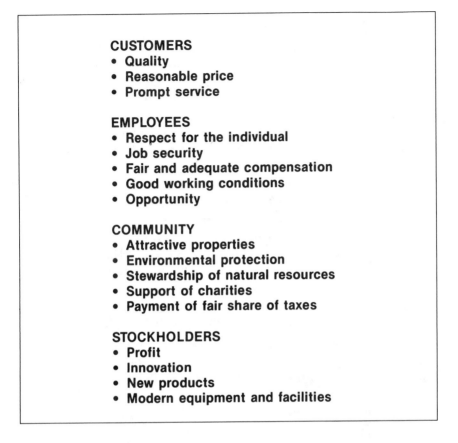

CUSTOMERS
- **Quality**
- **Reasonable price**
- **Prompt service**

EMPLOYEES
- **Respect for the individual**
- **Job security**
- **Fair and adequate compensation**
- **Good working conditions**
- **Opportunity**

COMMUNITY
- **Attractive properties**
- **Environmental protection**
- **Stewardship of natural resources**
- **Support of charities**
- **Payment of fair share of taxes**

STOCKHOLDERS
- **Profit**
- **Innovation**
- **New products**
- **Modern equipment and facilities**

Figure 27.   A summary of Johnson & Johnson values.

and to live the values on a daily basis — to "breathe life into them."

The principal mode of translating values into practice is through effective leadership. In the language of James MacGregor Burns, the challenge for each manager is to be a transforming leader: help raise your people from their lower selves to their higher selves. Help your people move up Maslow's hierarchy to self-esteem and self-actualization. When this is done, a beautiful thing happens. You will witness your people moving up the ladder of self-development from lower level values to higher level values. This is what transforming leadership is all about.

As a strategy for translating values into practice, you should focus on three interrelated avenues: balancing, communicating, and re-warding. We will look at each.

You can help your people move up Maslow's hierarchy by main-taining *a balanced view* of all the organizational values. The total set must be kept in proper perspective. When times are tough and it may be necessary to give special attention to one particular value (such as profitability), *do not lose sight of the others.* This demand for a balanced view requires that you be ever vigilant.

Here we can distinguish between the transactional leader and the transforming leader. The transactional leader will focus on measurable values — because they allow for a clear exchange of one thing for another. But the transforming leader will take these values for granted while at the same time attending to the more qualitative values. The transforming leader realizes the importance of all of the organizational values for the long-term success of the organization. These values are viewed as a set of interrelated elements, which means that the various values are mutually supportive and that no one of these values can be sacrificed without disrupting the total set.

As a leader, you should communicate the importance of the organizational values every day and at every opportunity. This com-munication may take a variety of forms: one-on-one communication, group meetings, written communication, and actions. Communica-tion takes place through both words and actions, and most would agree that actions or the absence thereof speak louder than words.

Whenever you are inquiring about performance — or simply, "How are things going?"—you should be especially attentive to the nature and scope of the questions. For instance, if the questions are limited to profitability, this restrictive interest will signal to your staff your principal, and perhaps only, priority. On the other hand, if your ques-tions are broadened to cover additional organizational values, this expansive interest will signal a very different set of priorities.

Similarly, whenever you present a report to your people on the group's performance, special attention should be given to the scope of the topics covered. If the progress report focuses only on bottom-line financial performance, the staff will clearly understand your sole priority. On the other hand, if such a presentation is expanded to cover progress on critical success factors associated with other organizational values, the staff will receive a completely different message. Communication is the key.

Considering a specific example of communication, all managers should bear in mind that the organization's reward system can also send a clear message to the staff communicating the relative importance of the organization's different values. What can a reward system include besides more pay and promotions? It also can include opportunity to receive further training, freedom to pursue a special interest, receipt of greater responsibility and authority, or simply hearing the supervisor remark, "That's great!"

A final consideration is the particular type of performance that is being rewarded. Are staff members rewarded only for being profitable? Or are they also rewarded for turning out quality products or services, for being innovative, for being good team players, for demonstrating high integrity, and for being good community citizens? We know from experience that the reward system is a powerful vehicle for communicating the organization's value system. The challenge for each manager is to use it effectively.

What does it all mean? Simply this: having a clear understanding of the organization's values — and a commitment to these values — will help the members of the organization make right-good decisions.

FORMULATING A CODE OF ETHICS

In a given organization, where should the promotion of ethics begin? Srivastva and Cooperrider state it well when they say:

> The promotion of ethics begins the day senior managers prepare an active and explicit position on the importance of the moral dimension in their organization.[117, p.18]

This active and explicit position on the importance of the moral dimension can best be presented in the form of a written code of ethics. The written code can communicate management's commitment to ethics and provide guidelines for decision making and action.

In a report entitled "Corporate Ethics," Ronald Berenbeim lists several reasons for a code of ethics:

1. Commitment of the chief executive officer
2. Maintenance of public trust and credibility
3. Greater managerial professionalism
4. Protection against improper employee conduct
5. Need to define ethical behavior in the light of new laws or social standards

6. Change in corporate culture or structure (decentralization, acquisition, and the like).[15, pp.13-14]

I have read numerous codes of ethics published by various companies. Some I would consider to be excellent, some are fair, and some are poor. It is important that managers understand the weaknesses inherent in some of these codes so that they do not repeat the mistakes of others.

It is clear that many codes of ethics are not grounded in a philosophical base. They are lacking a well-thought-out foundation. They often read as though they are simply a list of items that may have been generated in a brainstorming session without further scrutiny. As a consequence, the various items lack unity and coherence and are often contradictory in nature.

Some codes of ethics are too all-encompassing. They endeavor to "cover all bases" in a single document. They are not tailored to the particular needs of the various functional areas. As a consequence, any employee who reads the entire document might find that up to 80 percent of the information is irrelevant to his or her particular situation.

Other codes of ethics read as though they were formulated for the sole purpose of protecting the company. Certainly, protection can be one of the purposes of the document, but when survival becomes the sole purpose, many stakeholders are likely to be "turned off"— at least, will not be motivated to study the document in depth.

Consistent with the point immediately above, many codes are filled with legal jargon. They read as though written by a corporate lawyer. After reading the first few paragraphs of such a document, the typical employee is likely to set it aside for "later reading."

Then finally, a principal deficiency of many codes of ethics is their punitive tone throughout. The author or authors prefer to use "Thou shall not" rather than "Thou shalt." Grounded in a carrot-and-stick philosophy of motivation, these documents have lost sight of the carrot and raised the stick as the principal motivator. (Can such a document help lift people to their higher selves?)

These deficiencies are real — but they are not insurmountable. An effective leader-manager should be able to overcome each one and develop a code of ethics that will bear more fruit.

Our basic thesis here is that every organization should have a written code of ethics. And most important, every manager in the organization should understand the code of ethics and breathe life into it on a daily basis. It is not enough to simply *have* the document; it must become a reality in the daily lives of all employees.

What are the characteristics of a quality code of ethics? I would offer the following:

1. It is grounded in a philosophy of ethics.
2. It includes a generic code for all employees and also a focused code for each functional area.
3. It responds to the particular concerns of various stakeholders.
4. It is written in everyday language.
5. It is positive in tone.

Following these guidelines will not guarantee a perfect code of ethics, but it should promise one that is better than most.

Two illustrative codes of ethics are presented in Figure 28 and Figure 29. The first is intended as a generic code and would be disseminated to all employees in the company. The second is a focused code designed only for the marketing department and would be disseminated to all employees in that department. (This second code is adapted from the codes of ethics developed by these companies: General Dynamics, General Electric, Hewlett-Packard, IBM, Nash Finch Company, J. C. Penney, Pfizer, and Security Pacific Corporation.)

The question then becomes: How should an organization go about developing a code of ethics? A recommended strategy is presented in Figure 30. Underlying this recommended strategy are several salient assumptions. First, the code of ethics should be grounded in an explicit philosophy of ethics. Second, there is a need for both a generic code for the entire company as well as focused codes for the various functional areas. Third, the chief executive officer should play a major role in the entire process. And fourth, large numbers of managers should be given the opportunity to present their reactions and make suggestions regarding the draft code as it is being developed — which makes it a true participative process.

Implementing this recommended strategy should produce a code of ethics that will bear fruit. It should demonstrate a commitment to ethics on the part of upper management. It should establish a set of ground rules for determining appropriate and inappropriate behavior. And most important, it should help all managers make right-good decisions.

THE COMPANY CODE OF CONDUCT

1. We must conduct business in keeping with the highest moral, ethical, and legal standards.

2. We must maintain a workplace environment that encourages frank and open communications regarding matters of ethics.

3. We must be mindful that our commitment to ethical standards is absolute—it cannot be compromised.

4. We must always strive to make right-good decisions, "good" from a business standpoint and "right" from an ethical standpoint.

5. To determine if a decision is right or wrong, consider the likely consequences for all stakeholders.

6. To determine if a decision is right or wrong, consider the company's policies and procedures.

7. To determine if a decision is right or wrong, consider the company's values.

8. To determine if a decision is right or wrong, consider your own personal convictions.

9. In the final analysis, we will be judged by how well we made right-good decisions.

Figure 28.   A generic code of ethics.

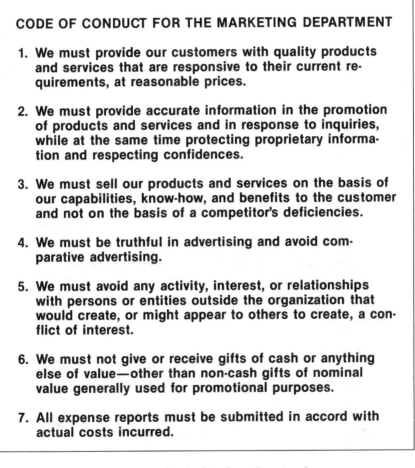

Figure 29.   A code of ethics for a functional area.

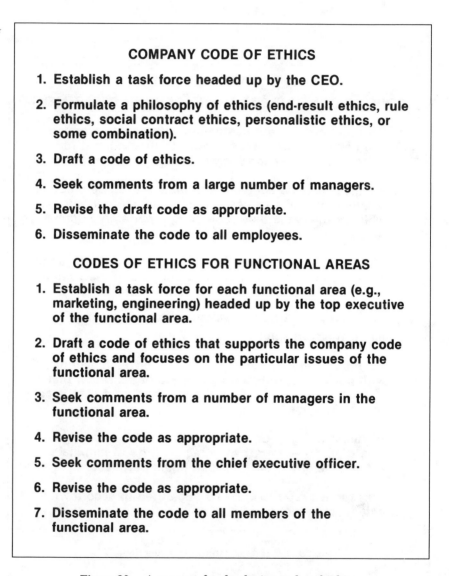

COMPANY CODE OF ETHICS

1. Establish a task force headed up by the CEO.

2. Formulate a philosophy of ethics (end-result ethics, rule ethics, social contract ethics, personalistic ethics, or some combination).

3. Draft a code of ethics.

4. Seek comments from a large number of managers.

5. Revise the draft code as appropriate.

6. Disseminate the code to all employees.

CODES OF ETHICS FOR FUNCTIONAL AREAS

1. Establish a task force for each functional area (e.g., marketing, engineering) headed up by the top executive of the functional area.

2. Draft a code of ethics that supports the company code of ethics and focuses on the particular issues of the functional area.

3. Seek comments from a number of managers in the functional area.

4. Revise the code as appropriate.

5. Seek comments from the chief executive officer.

6. Revise the code as appropriate.

7. Disseminate the code to all members of the functional area.

Figure 30.   A strategy for developing codes of ethics.

DEVELOPING AN ETHICS PROGRAM

Mark Pastin states it well when he says:

> Excellent companies do more than talk ethics. They take
> positive steps to address ethical issues and apply the prac-
> tical tools of ethics in their management practice.[99]

Our focus here is "putting theory into practice." We will now consider the practical steps that managers can take to make ethics a reality
in their organizations. The practical steps are integrated in the form
of an "ethics program."

The principal theme of our proposed ethics program is authentic communication. "What I have been urging, of course, is better
communication," says Barbara Ley Toffler. "Managers at all levels
of the organization and their employees must learn to *express* their
ethical concerns and *to listen to and hear* each other as they do so.
Without such effective exchange, the ethically best intentions are likely
to fall short of effective implementation."[119,p. 339]

Given the theme of authentic communication, our recommended
ethics program consists of the elements listed in Figure 31: (1) basic
information in the form of mission, values, and a code of ethics, (2)
an orientation program for new employees, (3) an ethics seminar for
managers, (4) participative decision making, (5) discussion of ethical
issues in management meetings, (6) an open door policy, and (7)
periodic ethics reviews. We will consider each.

1. Basic Information

The cornerstone of the ethics program would be basic information in the form of mission, values, and a code of ethics. These
three items would be developed for the organization as a whole
and then for each functional area. The mission, values, and code
of ethics for each functional area, of course, would support the
mission, values, and code of ethics for the larger organization.
This information should be organized in a small booklet that
would be disseminated to all employees.

2. Orientation Program for New Employees

All new employees deserve a good orientation program
regarding the organization as a whole as well as the functional
units within which they will work. These orientation sessions

---

1. **Basic information**
   - **Mission**
   - **Values**
   - **Code of ethics**

2. **Orientation of new employees**

3. **Ethics seminar for managers**

4. **Participative decision making**

5. **Ethics issues as an agenda item in meetings**

6. **An open door policy**

7. **Periodic ethics reviews**

Figure 31.   Elements of an ethics program.

should be viewed by management as an excellent opportunity to introduce new employees to corporate ethics — the basic ground rules for judging right and wrong conduct. It is highly desirable that the presentation on ethics at the company-wide orientation session be given by the chief executive. Similarly, the presentation on ethics at the functional level should be given by the head of the functional unit. A suggested outline for these two orientation sessions is presented in Figure 32. And remember: the law of primacy in learning tells us that people are likely to remember those things that they learn *at the very beginning.*

3. Ethics Seminar for Managers

Inasmuch as managers are the key agents for promoting ethical conduct throughout the organization, they should be well grounded in ethics. One approach is to schedule a multi-day seminar in "Ethics and Leadership"; its purpose would be to help

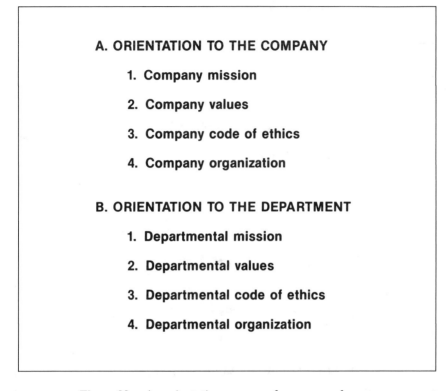

A. ORIENTATION TO THE COMPANY

    1. **Company mission**

    2. **Company values**

    3. **Company code of ethics**

    4. **Company organization**

B. ORIENTATION TO THE DEPARTMENT

    1. **Departmental mission**

    2. **Departmental values**

    3. **Departmental code of ethics**

    4. **Departmental organization**

Figure 32.   An orientation program for new employees.

managers: (1) understand ethics; (2) develop a framework for making ethical decisions; and (3) develop a plan of action for promoting ethical conduct in their organizational units. A suggested outline for such a seminar is shown in Figure 33. It would be important that these sessions be conducted in true seminar fashion — allowing for an open discussion of issues, dilemmas, and concerns.

The three-day seminars in business ethics conducted at Allied Corporation apparently have been well received. They have been reported on by David Freudberg:

> The three-day seminars in business ethics at Allied Corporation, held at a well-appointed retreat center, have to date been attended by some four hundred middle managers at Allied.
> Participants prepare anonymous cases from direct

A SEMINAR IN ETHICS AND LEADERSHIP

Day 1

1. **The importance of ethics**

2. **Ethical dilemmas**

Day 2

3. **The corporate philosophy of ethics**

4. **The corporate code of ethics**

Day 3

5. **The effective leader**

6. **What should be done**

Figure 33. Outline of an ethics seminar for managers

on-the-job experiences in which choosing the ethically "right" thing to do proved a difficult decision. In analyzing these examples, the seminar offers a "suggested pattern of inquiry" by which managers can weigh their responsibilities in light of the facts, the affected parties, and the necessary authority to carry out what is deemed correct.[39, p.45]

4. Participative Decision Making

In making a decision, there are two radically different approaches that a manager might use. The Lone Ranger approach involves a leader acting on a solo basis in making the decision and then instructing the staff to carry it out. The participative approach involves the leader in soliciting ideas from others during the decision making process and then incorporating the ideas as appropriate. When a decision involves an ethical issue, the second approach is recommended. As the old adage goes: "Two heads are better than one." It should be noted that, with regard to accountability for the outcome of the decision, the participative approach does not relieve the manager one iota. Nevertheless, a participative approach should increase the likelihood of a right-good decision.

The participative approach to decision making calls for complete openness and candor. In a paper entitled "The Perils of Accord," Warren Bennis stresses the importance of "creative confrontation":

> I think that too much accord is always perilous and usually false. Two of this country's most effective executives — Jim Burke at Johnson & Johnson and Andrew Grover at Intel — insist on what they describe as "creative confrontation" with their associates. They not only encourage dissent in the executive suite, they demand it and surround themselves with people smart enough to know the truth and independent enough to speak it — especially when it's at apparent odds with their own perceptions.[12]

5. Discussion of Ethical Issues in Management Meetings

Managers have the opportunity to create an environment that will help surface ethical issues during the normal course of events. A practical suggestion would be to include "Ethical Issues" as an agenda item in staff meetings. That way, every team member should feel free to bring up for discussion any ethical concern or issue that might have arisen since the last meeting and discuss it with the entire team.

Here we also should remember that "Almost any problem in the world could have been solved if it had been dealt with when it was a *small* problem."

6. An Open Door Policy

As a means of reducing the need for whistle blowing, Kenneth Walters offers some practical suggestions:

- Encourage an open environment in which employees can freely express their often controversial views.
- Establish a sincere "open door" policy that allows employees to get a direct and sympathetic hearing on issues of concern to them.
- Keep the channels of communication open on the large questions of corporate social policy and social responsibility.
- Formally recognize and communicate to employees a respect for the individual consciences of employees.
- Respect an employee's right to differ with organizational policy on some matters.[123]

The important thing to appreciate from these words of advice is that an "open door" policy does not merely refer to the door's actual position. Rather, it refers to an organizational culture and climate that allows — and encourages — an open exchange of ideas and concerns. This open exchange captures the true meaning of the word "communicate"— to commune, to share. A climate of openness that fosters authentic communication is essential to the success of an ethics program.

7. Periodic Ethics Reviews

Here we question, "What you don't know won't hurt you." Envision a situation where some stakeholders have serious reservations about the integrity of your organization or organizational unit — and you are not aware of these reservations. You could be in for serious trouble. In fact, this lack of information could prove fatal.

How might a manager stay abreast of how people view the level of integrity of his or her organization or organizational unit? A practical approach would be to conduct an annual ethics review.

The review would involve administering a brief questionnaire to at least a sample of all stakeholder groups — customers, suppliers, upper management, peer groups, and staff. The questionnaire would cover the basic principles included in the code of ethics. Each respondent would be asked to evaluate (on a five-point scale) how well the organization or organizational unit is satisfying the intent of each principle. The questionnaire should be completed and returned anonymously.

Analyzing the results of the survey should give the manager

meaningful baseline data regarding how the various stakeholder groups perceive his or her organization or organizational unit in terms of ethical conduct. And if some of the scores are found to be medium to low, this should not be reason for despair — but reason for problem solving and corrective action.

Implementing a program such as that outlined here could have a profound impact on any organization. By incorporating ethics as an integral part of the management function, the organization could be lifted to its "higher self"—that is, to higher levels of ethics and morality.

It is important to note that some version of the recommended ethics program could be initiated at any level of management — from chief executive officer down to department manager. In many organizations, it is not necessary for all managers to simply "stand by" and wait for the CEO to initiate an ethics program. Precisely what actions a particular manager might take would depend, of course, on the freedom and authority of the manager. Given this qualifying remark, it is reasonable for each manager to consider what might be done to initiate an ethics program in his or her organizational unit.

It also is important to note that the initiation of an ethics program is not without risk. If this happens to be the very first time that ethical issues have been discussed openly, perhaps some long-forgotten skeletons will emerge from the closet. What if some of these skeletons are the sole possession of one or more present members of upper management? Suppose that some activity is uncovered that is both unethical and illegal. What then? These questions are not presented as scare tactics but simply as real concerns that should help keep us close to reality.

Assuming that the skeletons can be dealt with, then the organization should be able to move forward in its efforts to include ethics as an integral part of its overall strategy. As it moves forward, it should move up the ethics scale — because all managers in the organization should have the basic tools needed for making right-good decisions.

SUMMING UP

Let's suppose that you, as a leader-manager, have been successful in implementing an ethics program in your organizational unit. You have developed a strategy for making ethical decisions, and you apply the strategy on a day-to-day basis. You have developed a plan of action for promoting ethical conduct in your unit, and you have carried through on the plan. As a consequence of these actions, you find that your unit is operating in a highly ethical manner. And importantly, you are viewed by your people as a person of integrity — as a truly ethical person.

We now ask: What are the implications of these actions and events? One answer, of course, is that there is no need to look higher or further, because integrity — the good life — is an end in itself. But the pragmatist is more demanding. This very practical and results-oriented person insists on a response that can shed light on the *consequences* of ethical conduct.

Well, we need not withdraw from the question. We can respond to the pragmatist with a definitive answer: *ethical conduct generates trust.* Trust has been described as the "miracle ingredient"— the glue that holds a group together. Without the glue, there will be no common bond among the members of the group. It is no simple matter to define trust, but *we know it when we experience it.*

Imagine a situation in which there is lack of trust. Take Jethro, for example, a middle-level manager who has 100 people in his department and four section managers reporting to him. Jethro has a great deal in his favor: he is technically competent, he has a clear vision for the department, and he is strongly committed to achieving the vision. But Jethro has one major deficiency: he is found lacking in integrity.

These are some of Jethro's symptoms. First, he is seldom convincing when talking to his people on a given matter. Second, he often will say one thing and then do something to the contrary — he does not "walk the talk." Further, he frequently gets caught up in contradictions — he will say one thing to one person and something contradictory to another. We would be hard pressed to identify the basic values from which Jethro is operating. His actions do not appear to be guided by any coherent set of principles. As a consequence of all of this, Jethro's people simply do not trust him.

Given the makeup of Jethro's behavior, do you think that he will be able to lift his people to their higher selves? Certainly not. The best that we might expect is that his followers will maintain their status quo. And the worst-case scenario is that he will take them down to their lower selves. In either case, the lack of effective leadership — caused by Jethro's lack of integrity — will be a definite impediment to both Jethro and the department.

The long-term implications of Jethro's character and conduct are discouraging. His section managers will spend a great deal of time just trying to figure out where Jethro is "coming from" and what he's likely to do next. The high achievers will soon grow weary of this unproductive use of their time and will leave. Those who remain will do just enough to retain their jobs — no more and no less. What a pity! If earlier in his career, Jethro had had a good coach or mentor who could have pointed him in the right-good direction, he probably would not be in his present predicament.

Our basic thesis here is that effective leadership is grounded in trust. Leadership is a *relationship* between leader and follower. The leadership function is not found solely within the leader, nor is it found solely within the followers. Leadership transcends both the leader per se and the followers per se. And we can strongly affirm that this relationship is based upon trust. Without trust, there can be no effective relationship. And without the relationship, there can be no effective leadership.

The person aspiring to be an effective leader-manager asks: How does this trust come about? Good question. We can give no cookbook answer, but we can offer some general guidelines.

Trust cannot be demanded; it must be earned. Trust is earned by being sincere. It is earned by being dependable, by being a person of your word. It is earned by "walking the talk." It is earned by owning up to your mistakes. It is earned by being willing to say "I don't know." Essentially, it is earned by being honest. This is what the building of trust is all about.

This building of trust between leader and follower does not occur "over night." It takes time to build the trust — and a much shorter time to destroy it. A trusting relationship is both precious and fragile.

The person aspiring to be an effective leader-manager then asks: What actions should I take to assure that I am building a trusting relationship with my people? Another good question. And again, there is no cookbook answer, but there is one principal guideline.

The only possible way to build the trust of your people is for them to trust you. The only way to achieve this trust is *to be authentic.* Be "for real"; don't be a phony.

Authenticity is the relationship between one's inner self and one's outer self. Your inner self is your innermost being that looks out at the world. Only you know your inner self. Your outer self is the image that you project to others. It is how others see you. You are an authentic person to the extent that your outer self is an accurate representation of your inner self. In other words, the two selves are in harmony.

Abraham Maslow defines authenticity in terms of "phoniness being reduced toward the zero point." As phoniness is reduced toward the zero point, we observe a beautiful thing happening in both ourselves and others: an obvious increase in openness, candor, frankness, and directness. These outcomes are no mean achievement.

If, over the years, you have been merely pretending, it will not be easy to start being authentic. As William James noted, habits start out as cobwebs and eventually become cables. The breaking of cables is no simple matter. But if one wants to generate trust, one must begin.

In sum, we have defined leadership in terms of a relationship between leader and follower. This relationship is based upon trust, and trust is generated by being a person of integrity. The hallmark of the entire process is authenticity.

The causal chain can be elucidated in terms of a syllogism:
- Trust is required for effective leadership.
- Without personal integrity, there can be no mutual trust.
- Therefore, without personal integrity, there can be no effective leadership.

At this point in the argument, the pragmatist once again enters the picture. Our results-oriented friend poses this question: Will integrity assure effective leadership?

Good question, and there is a clear answer: to be an effective leader, integrity is necessary but not sufficient. To reach the top of the mountain, integrity must be combined with competence, vision, and enthusiasm. Of these four traits, integrity is the foundation. Integrity is the base of the pyramid on which the other three traits rest. Take away the base and the pyramid will collapse. But given a solid base, we have a foundation on which to establish effective leadership. That's it in a nutshell.

Final Summing Up

Go to the end and then stop.

from *Alice in Wonderland*

Anyone attending a Shakespearean play back in seventeenth-century England would be assisted in understanding the play. First, the narrator would come out on the stage and tell the audience what the play is all about. Next, the play would be presented. And finally, after the last act, the narrator would reappear and summarize the key points of the play.

Our epic drama on ethics and leadership — with the hero being the transforming leader — is now concluded. The synopsis will be in the form of ten guiding principles, which will serve as a review and a reminder for what has been said.

1. **Ethics plays an important role in both the short-term success and the long-term success of an organization.**

   Many would argue that being ethical should not be viewed merely as a means to something else, but is an end in itself (and I would concur). But the pragmatist is overly demanding in wanting to know the *practical consequences* of ethical conduct. We can reply to the pragmatist that the organization that is both competent and ethical is more likely to succeed than the organization that is merely competent. The former organization has the "ethics edge," and this edge, though subtle, is not trivial.

2. **The variation in the ethical conduct of the members of an**

207

organization is influenced primarily by the managers of the organization.

It is much more realistic to view ethical conduct in terms of a continuum (say, a 1-to-10 scale) than in terms of a binary scale (i.e., ethical and unethical). This does not mean that ethical standards should vary but only that, in fact, behavior of individuals does vary. Ethical conduct varies from person to person, and it varies within a person from day to day and from situation to situation. An individual's nodal point on the continuum is a function of background, but the variation around the nodal point is influenced primarily by the individual's managers. We know that other factors are important — such as the type of industry, the behavior of peers, and the moral climate of the nation — but the most important factor is the climate or culture created by the organization's managers.

3. **Ethics is grounded in values — the enduring beliefs that guide one's conduct.**

To understand a person's ethics, it is necessary to understand the person's values. The values are the enduring beliefs or ground rules by which a person guides his or her life. The set of values constitutes the core of one's ethical system. One's ethics can be judged on the basis of two types of consistency: (1) Are the values themselves internally consistent (i.e., mutually supportive)? and (2) Is the individual's behavior consistent with the stated values? These notions about values and consistency apply to both the individual and the organization.

4. **Ethical dilemmas arise as a result of conflict in values.**

If ethics were only a matter of choosing between right and wrong, a manager's life would be fairly simple. But not so. Frequently, the choice is between two wrongs. And often it is a matter of choosing between an alternative that is "good" from an economic or business standpoint and one that is "right" from an ethics standpoint. Managers face such dilemmas day in and day out, and being able to deal with these dilemmas in an acceptable manner — i.e., by making right-good decisions — is one of the greatest challenges of management.

5. **The person of true integrity — the one who is best able to resolve ethical dilemmas — lives out of the Encompassing.**

Karl Jaspers' idea of the Encompassing provides a sound framework for formulating a theory of ethics that can help managers make ethical decisions. The Encompassing includes four levels of being — empirical existence, consciousness at large, spirit, and Existenz — with the connecting bond being reason. The higher levels of being include and give direction to the lower levels. Humans are endowed with the potential for achieving the level of Existenz, but many get stuck at lower levels of being. The person who does not get stuck at a lower level and achieves the level of Existenz may be viewed as a "fully functioning person"— or, as Aristotle might say, a person who has achieved "the good life." The fully functioning person, the one who lives out of the Encompassing, may be viewed as the person of true integrity.

6. **The Encompassing theory of ethics — which incorporates four ethical systems and is guided by reason — provides a theoretical framework for making right-good decisions.**

The four levels of being have their counterparts in four distinct systems of ethics. This is the alignment:
- Empirical existence — end-result ethics
- Consciousness at large — rule ethics
- Spirit — social contract ethics
- Existenz — personalistic ethics.

Each of these ethical systems has a different locus of authority:
- End-result ethics — expected consequences
- Rule ethics — laws and commandments
- Social contract ethics — customs and norms
- Personalistic ethics — one's conscience.

Inasmuch as the person of true integrity is defined as one who lives out of the Encompassing, it follows that, in an effort to make right-good decisions, this person will make use of all four ethical systems. In practice, it means giving due consideration to expected consequences, rules and laws, customs and norms of the community, and one's personal convictions — with the entire process being guided by reason.

7. **The Encompassing theory of leadership — which gives due consideration to four different leadership styles — places the transforming leader at the top rung of the ladder.**

The four different ethical systems find their counterparts in four distinct leadership styles. This is the alignment:
- End-result ethics — the manipulator
- Rule ethics — the bureaucratic administrator
- Social contract ethics — the professional manager
- Personalistic ethics — the transforming leader.

Each leadership style has a different view of its principal function:
- Manipulative leadership — to use power and cunning to further one's own ends.
- Bureaucratic administration — to communicate and enforce rules.
- Professional management — to make decisions regarding human, material, and financial resources for the purpose of achieving organizational objectives.
- Transforming leadership — to empower followers by lifting them to their higher selves.

The transforming leader, who lives out of the Encompassing and is guided by the Encompassing theory of ethics, makes use of the *desirable features* of all four leadership styles. This leader understands the importance of power, the need for structure and systems, and the importance of managing resources for the purpose of achieving organizational objectives. But most important, the transforming leader realizes that the principal function of leadership is *leading people.*

8. **The Encompassing decision making strategy — which is grounded in the Encompassing theory of ethics — provides a practical framework for making right-good decisions.**

In most cases, the manager who is guided by a decision making strategy will make better decisions than the manager who has no such strategy for guidance. Most managers have been exposed to decision making strategies that focus on the economic or business aspects of their jobs. But relatively few have been exposed to strategies that focus on the ethical aspects of their jobs. And a smaller number have been exposed to a strategy that incorporates both the economic dimension and the ethics dimension. It is this incorporation of both dimensions that the Encompassing decision making strategy accomplishes.

After the objective or problem is stated, the strategy calls for these four steps.

1. Test for expected results
2. Test for organizational policies and procedures
3. Test for organizational values
4. Test for personal conviction.

Cutting through all of these tests is the use of reason. Applying this strategy in a thoughtful manner should lead to right-good decisions.

9. **The Encompassing ethics plan can help promote ethical conduct throughout the organization.**

Ethical conduct among the members of an organization is not something that will simply "happen." Nor can it be taken for granted. The likelihood of ethical conduct can be enhanced through specific actions.

To this end, we have proposed a comprehensive ethics plan that includes these elements:

1. Basic information (mission, values, and code of ethics)
2. An orientation program for new employees
3. An ethics seminar for managers
4. Participative decision making
5. An open door policy
6. Including "Ethical Issues" as an agenda item in staff meetings
7. A periodic ethics review.

Carrying through on this plan would help managers promote ethical conduct on the part of their people and should lead to a higher percentage of right-good decisions.

10. **Integrity, trust, and effective leadership are interconnected in a causal chain.**

The relations between and among integrity, trust, and effective leadership are evident. We know that, on the down side, lack of integrity on the part of the leader will lead to lack of trust, which will lead to ineffective leadership. But we also know that, on the up side, integrity on the part of the leader will lead to trust, which will contribute to effective leadership. We say "contribute to" because integrity is necessary but not sufficient. It must be combined with competence, vision, and enthusiasm to "lead to" effective leadership. But the foundation of the pyramid is integrity — without which the pyramid will collapse.

We have now come to the end of our story. I would like to close with the following challenge that Michael Josephson, a Loyola Marymount ethicist, presents to each and to all:

> The notion that nice guys finish last is not only poisonous but wrong. In fact, the contrary is true. Unethical conduct is always self-destructive and generates more unethical conduct until you hit the pits. The challenge is not always being ethical or paying a big price. The challenge is to be ethical and get what you want. I think you can do it almost every time.[61]

In sum, the challenge is to be ever mindful of making right-good decisions.

Appendix

EXERCISES

I. THE IMPORTANCE OF VALUES

Select those values in the two Rokeach lists (in Chapter I) that are of most importance to you.

A. List your top five terminal values:

-
-
-
-
-

B. List your top five instrumental values:

-
-
-
-
-

C. Check the ten values for internal consistency. Do they constitute a unified set?

II. CONFLICT IN VALUES

Describe a work-related ethical dilemma (involving a conflict in values) that you have faced.

III. THE GOOD LIFE

Write a personal profile of yourself in terms of the four levels of being.

- **Empirical existence** (job, family, hobbies):

- **Consciousness at large** (specific areas of knowledge):

- **Spirit** (leading ideas that guide your life):

- **Existenz** (distinguishing attributes that make you a unique person):

IV. ETHICAL SYSTEMS

Building on the principles underlying the four ethical systems presented in Chapter IV, outline your personal ethical system in terms of guiding principles.

V. LEADERSHIP STYLES

Building on the principles underlying the four leadership styles presented in Chapter V, outline your philosophy of leadership in terms of guiding principles.

VI. WHAT SHOULD BE DONE

Development of a Plan of Action for Promoting Ethical Conduct

A. Purpose

1. What is the mission of the larger organization of which you are a part?

2. What is the mission of your organizational unit?

B. Values

1. What are the principal values of the larger organization of which you are a part?

2. What are the principal values that you want to promote in your organizational unit?

C. Code of Ethics

Formulate a code of ethics for your organizational unit in the form of ten guiding principles.

1.

2.

3.

4.

5.

6.

7.

8.

9.

10.

D. Developing an Ethics Program

Outline what you would include in an ethics program for promoting ethical conduct in your unit. (Consider the following possibilities: orientation program for new employees, ethics seminar for managers, participative decision making, open door policy, including "Ethics Issues" as an agenda item in staff meetings, and an annual ethics review.)

Suggested Readings

Bibliography

1. Adler, Norman. "The Sounds of Executive Silence." *Harvard Business Review*, July–August 1971.
2. Appley, Lawrence. *Management in Action: The Art of Getting Things Done Through People.* New York: American Management Association, 1956.
3. Appley, Lawrence. *The Management Evolution.* New York: American Management Association, 1963.
4. Appley, Lawrence. *Values in Management.* New York: American Management Association, 1969.
5. Aristotle. *The Nicomachean Ethics.* Buffalo, New York: Prometheus Books, 1987.
6. Atlantic Council of the United States. "The Teaching of Values and the Successor Generation." Washington, D. C., 1983.
7. Austin, Robert. "Code of Conduct for Executives." *Harvard Business Review*, Sept.–Oct. 1961.
8. Baumhart, Raymond. *An Honest Profit.* New York: Holt, Rinehart and Winston, 1968.
9. Bellah, Robert, Richard Madsen, William Sullivan, Ann Swidler, and Steven Tipton. *Habits of the Heart: Individualism and Commitment in American Life.* Berkeley, California: University of California Press, 1985.
10. Bennis, Warren. "Conversation with Warren Bennis." In *Effective Management and the Behavioral Sciences*, William Dowling (Ed). New York: AMACOM, a Division of the American Management Associations, 1978.
11. Bennis, Warren. "The Cannibals Among Us." *New Management*, Spring 1987.

12. Bennis, Warren. "The Perils of Accord." *New Management,* Summer 1987.
13. Bennis, Warren, and Burt Nanus. *Leaders: The Strategies for Taking Charge.* New York: Harper & Row, 1985.
14. Bentham, Jeremy. *An Introduction to the Principles of Morals and Legislation.* Oxford: Oxford Press, 1789.
15. Berenbeim, Ronald. "Corporate Ethics." A Research Report from the Conference Board, 1987.
16. Berney, Karen. "Finding the Ethical Edge." *Nation's Business,* August 1987.
17. Bhambri, Arvind, and Jeffrey Sonnenfeld. "The Man Who Stands Alone." *New Management,* Spring 1987.
18. Bowen, Ezra. "Looking to Its Roots." *Time,* May 25, 1987.
19. Brenner, Steven, and Earl Molander. "Is the Ethics of Business Changing?" *Harvard Business Review,* Jan.–Feb. 1977.
20. Buber, Martin. *Between Man and Man.* Boston: Beacon Press, 1955.
21. Buber, Martin. *Eclipse of God.* New York: Harper & Row, 1952.
22. Buber, Martin. *I and Thou.* New York: Charles Scribner's Sons, 1958.
23. Buber, Martin. *Israel and the World: Essays in a Time of Crisis.* New York: Schocken Books, 1963.
24. Buber, Martin. *Pointing the Way.* New York: Harper & Row, 1963.
25. Buber, Martin. *Ten Rungs: Hasidic Sayings.* New York: Schocken Books, 1962.
26. Burns, James MacGregor. *Leadership.* New York: Harper & Row, 1978.
27. Cadbury, Sir Adrian. "Ethical Managers Make Their Own Rules." *Harvard Business Review,* Sept.–Oct. 1987.
28. Carr, Albert. "Can an Executive Afford a Conscience?" *Harvard Business Review,* July–August 1970.
29. Davis, Stanley. *Managing Corporate Culture.* Cambridge, Massachusetts: Ballinger Publishing Company, 1984.
30. Deal, Terrence, and Allan Kennedy. *Corporate Cultures: The Rites and Rituals of Corporate Life.* Reading, Massachusetts: Addison-Wesley, 1982.
31. Drucker, Peter. *The Effective Executive.* New York: Harper & Row, 1967.

32. Drucker, Peter. *Management: Tasks • Responsibilities • Practices.* New York: Harper & Row, 1973.
33. Dyer, William. *Contemporary Issues in Management and Organization Development.* Reading, Massachusetts: Addison-Wesley, 1983.
34. Ehrlich, Leonard, Edith Ehrlich, and George Pepper (Eds.) *Karl Jaspers: Basic Philosophical Writings.* Athens, Ohio: Ohio University Press, 1986.
35. Elbing, Alvar, and Carol Elbing. *The Value Issues of Business.* New York: McGraw-Hill Book Company, 1967.
36. Emerson, Ralph Waldo. *Essays and Lectures.* New York: The Library of America, 1983.
37. England, George. "Personal Value Systems of American Managers." *Academy of Management,* March 1967.
38. Fendrock, John. "Crisis of Conscience at Quasar." *Harvard Business Review,* March–April 1968.
39. Freudberg, David. *The Corporate Conscience.* New York: AMACOM, a Division of American Management Association, 1986.
40. Fromm, Erich. *Man for Himself: An Inquiry into the Psychology of Ethics.* New York: Fawcett World Library, 1947.
41. Gantt, Henry. *Organizing for Work.* New York: Harcourt, Brace & Howe, 1919.
42. Gellerman, Saul. *Motivation and Productivity.* New York: American Management Associations, 1963.
43. Gellerman, Saul. "Why 'Good' Managers Make Bad Ethical Choices." *Harvard Business Review,* July–August 1986.
44. Gerth, H. H., and C. Wright Mills (Eds.) *From Max Weber: Essays in Sociology.* New York: Oxford University Press, 1946.
45. Gilbreath, Robert. "The Hollow Executive." *New Management,* Spring 1987.
46. Goodpaster, Kenneth. "Should Sponsors Screen for Moral Values?" *The Hastings Center Report,* Dec. 1983.
47. Greyser, Stephen, and Bonnie Reece. "Businessmen Look Hard at Advertising." *Harvard Business Review,* May–June 1971.
48. Guth, William, and Renato Tagiuri. "Personal Values and Corporate Strategy." *Harvard Business Review,* Sept.–Oct. 1965.
49. Harrison, Roger. "Harnessing Personal Energy: How Companies Can Inspire Employees." *Organizational Dynamics,* Autumn 1987.

50. Harrison, Roger. "Quality of Service: A New Frontier for Integrity in Organizations." In *Executive Integrity*, by Suresh Srivastra and Associates.

51. Hill, Gladwin. "The Shifting Sands of Public Consent." *New Management*, Spring 1987.

52. Horton, Thomas. "Shaping Business Values." *Management Review*, April 1984.

53. Horton, Thomas. *"What Works for Me": 16 CEOs Talk About Their Careers and Commitments*. New York: Random House, 1986.

54. Jackall, Robert. "Moral Mazes: Bureaucracy and Managerial Work." *Harvard Business Review*, Sept.–Oct. 1983.

55. Jaspers, Karl. *The Future of Mankind*. Chicago: The University of Chicago Press, 1961.

56. Jaspers, Karl. *Philosophy* (II). Chicago: The University of Chicago Press, 1969.

57. Jaspers, Karl. *Philosophy of Existence*. Philadelphia: University of Pennsylvania Press, 1971.

58. Jaspers, Karl. *The Question of German Guilt*. New York: Dial Press, 1947.

59. Jaspers, Karl. *Reason and Existenz*. New York: The Noonday Press, 1955.

60. Jaspers, Karl. *Von der Wahrheit*. Translations in Ehrlich, Ehrlich, and Pepper.

61. Josephson, Michael. Quoted in "Ethics: Looking at Its Roots," by Ezra Bowen. *Time*, May 25, 1987.

62. Jowett, B. (Ed.). *The Dialogues of Plato*. New York: Random House, 1920.

63. Kant, Immanuel. *Critique of Practical Reason*. New York: The Bobbs-Merrill Company, 1956.

64. Kant, Immanuel. *Groundwork of the Metaphysic of Morals*. New York: Harper & Row, 1964.

65. Kant, Immanuel. *Lectures on Ethics*. New York: Harper & Row, 1963.

66. Kant, Immanuel. *Religion Within the Limits of Reason Alone*. New York: Harper & Row, 1960.

67. Katz, Daniel, and Robert Kahn. *The Social Psychology of Organizations*. New York: John Wiley & Sons, 1978.

68. Katz, Robert. "Toward a More Effective Enterprise." *Harvard Business Review*, Sept.–Oct. 1960.

69. Kelen, Emery (Ed.) *Hammarskjold: The Political Man.* New York: Funk & Wagnalls Publishing Company, 1968.
70. Kerr, Steven. "Integrity in Effective Leadership." In *Executive Integrity*, by Suresh Srivastra and Associates.
71. Kolb, David. "Integrity, Advanced Professional Development, and Learning." In *Executive Integrity*, by Suresh Srivastra and Associates.
72. Koontz, Harold, Cyril O'Donnell, and Heinz Weihrich. *Management.* New York: McGraw-Hill, 1980.
73. Kouzes, James, and Barry Posner. *The Leadership Challenge: How to Get Extraordinary Things Done in Organizations.* San Francisco: Jossey-Bass Publishers, 1987.
74. Kristol, Irvin. "Ethics, Anyone? Or Morals?" *The Wall Street Journal*, Sept. 15, 1987.
75. Lecky, Prescott. "The Personality." In *The Self: Explorations in Personal Growth*, Clark Moustakas (Ed.). New York: Harper & Row, 1956.
76. Lin, Yutang. *The Pleasures of a Nonconformist.* Cleveland, Ohio: The World Publishing Company, 1962.
77. Machiavelli, Niccolò. *The Prince.* New York: The New American Library, 1980.
78. MacIntyre, Alasdair. *A Short History of Ethics.* New York: Macmillan Publishing Company, 1966.
79. Mackie, John. *Ethics: Inventing Right and Wrong.* New York: Viking Penguin, 1977.
80. Maslow, Abraham. *Eupsychian Management.* Homewood, Illinois: Richard D. Irwin, 1965.
81. Maslow, Abraham. *Toward a Psychology of Being.* New York: Van Nostrand Reinhold, 1968.
82. Matthews, John, Kenneth Goodpaster, and Laura Nash. *Policies and Persons: A Casebook in Business Ethics.* New York: McGraw-Hill Book Company, 1985.
83. May, William. "Good Ethics is Good Business." *New Management*, Spring 1987.
84. McCloy, John. "On Corporate Payoffs." *Harvard Business Review*, July–August 1976.
85. McCoy, Bowen. "The Parable of the Sadhu." *Harvard Business Review*, Sept.–Oct. 1983.
86. McMurry, Robert. "Conflicts in Human Values." *Harvard Business Review*, May–June 1963.

87. McMurry, Robert. "Power and the Ambitious Executive." *Harvard Business Review*, Nov.–Dec. 1973.

88. Mill, John Stuart. *Utilitarianism, On Liberty, Essay on Bentham*. New York: New American Library, 1962.

89. Miller, Samuel. "The Tangle of Ethics." *Harvard Business Review*, Jan.–Feb. 1960.

90. Mintzberg, Henry. *The Nature of Managerial Work*. Englewood Cliffs, New Jersey: Prentice-Hall, 1980.

91. Moustakas, Clark (Ed.). *The Self: Explorations in Personal Growth*. New York: Harper & Row, Publishers, 1956.

92. Myers, David. "A Psychology of Evil." *The Other Side*, April 1982.

93. Nash, Laura. "Ethics Without the Sermon." *Harvard Business Review*, Nov.–Dec. 1981.

94. Odiorne, George. *MBO II: A System of Managerial Leadership for the 80s*. Belmont, California: Fearon Pitman Publishers, 1979.

95. Ohmann, O. A. "Skyhooks." *Harvard Business Review*. May–June 1955.

96. Ouchi, William. *Theory Z: How American Business Can Meet the Japanese Challenge*. Reading, Massachusetts: Addison-Wesley, 1981.

97. Pascale, Richard, and Anthony Athos. *The Art of Japanese Management: Applications for American Executives*. New York: Simon and Schuster, 1981.

98. Pastin, Mark. "A Code of Ethics for Your Organization." An unpublished paper, March 31, 1987.

99. Pastin, Mark. "Ethics and Excellence." *New Management*, Spring 1987.

100. Pastin, Mark. *The Hard Problems of Management: Gaining the Ethics Edge*. San Francisco: Jossey-Bass Publishers, 1986.

101. Peck, M. Scott. *The Road Less Traveled*. New York: Simon and Schuster, 1978.

102. Peters, Thomas, and Robert Waterman. *In Search of Excellence: Lessons from America's Best-Run Companies*. New York: Harper & Row, 1982.

103. Rest, James. *Moral Development: Advances in Research and Theory*. New York: Praeger Publishers, 1986.

104. Rokeach, Milton. *The Nature of Human Values*. New York: The Free Press, 1973.

105. Roosevelt, Franklin. "Four Freedoms" *Speech*, Jan. 6, 1941.
106. Rousseau, Jean Jacques. *The Social Contract.* New York: Hafner Publishing Company, 1947.
107. Russell, Bertrand. *Power.* New York: W. W. Norton & Company, 1966.
108. Russell, Bertrand. *Philosophical Essays.* New York: Simon and Schuster, 1966.
109. Schilpp, Paul (Ed.) *The Philosophy of Karl Jaspers.* New York: Tudor Publishing Company, 1957.
110. Schmidt, Warren, and Barry Posner. *Managerial Values in Perspective.* New York: American Management Associations, 1983.
111. Sethi, S. Prakash. "The Multinational Challenge." *New Management*, Spring 1987.
112. Shea, Gordon. *Building Trust in the Workplace.* New York: American Management Associations, 1984.
113. Sheldon, Oliver. *The Philosophy of Management.* London: Pitman, 1923.
114. Sherwin, Douglas. "The Ethical Roots of the Business System." *Harvard Business Review*, Nov.–Dec. 1983.
115. Silk, Leonard, and David Vogel. *Ethics and Profits: The Crisis of Confidence in American Business.* New York: Simon and Schuster, 1976.
116. Solomon, Robert, and Kristine Hanson. *Above the Bottom Line: An Introduction to Business Ethics.* New York: Harcourt Brace Jovanovich, 1983.
117. Srivastva, Suresh, and Associates. *Executive Integrity: The Search for High Human Values in Organizational Life.* San Francisco: Jossey-Bass Publishers, 1988.
118. Thiroux, Jacques. *Ethics: Theory and Practice.* New York: Macmillan, 1986.
119. Toffler, Barbara Ley. *Tough Choices.* New York: John Wiley & Sons, 1986.
120. Velasquez, Manuel. *Business Ethics: Concepts and Cases.* Englewood Cliffs, New Jersey: Prentice-Hall, 1982.
121. Wall, Jerry. "What the Competition is Doing: Your Need to Know." *Harvard Business Review*, Nov.–Dec. 1974.
122. Wallraff, Charles. *Karl Jaspers: An Introduction to His Philosophy.* Princeton, New Jersey: Princeton University Press, 1970.
123. Walters, Kenneth. "Your Employees' Right to Blow the Whistle." *Harvard Business Review*, July–August 1975.

124. Warnock, G. J. *Contemporary Moral Philosophy.* New York: St. Martin's Press, 1967.
125. Weber, Max. "Bureaucracy." In *From Max Weber: Essays in Sociology,* H. H. Gerth and C. Wright Mills (Eds.). New York: Oxford University Press, 1958.
126. Whyte, William H. Jr. *The Organization Man.* New York: Simon and Schuster, 1956.
127. Williams, Bernard. *Ethics and the Limits of Philosophy.* Cambridge, Massachusetts: Harvard University Press, 1985.
128. Wolfe, Donald. "Is There Integrity in the Bottom Line?" In *Executive Integrity: The Search for High Human Values in Organizational Life* by Srivastra and Associates.
129. Wolff, Robert Paul. *About Philosophy.* Englewood Cliffs, New Jersey: Prentice-Hall, 1981.

Author Index

233

Subject Index